Yet Not Forsaken

Rising up from the ashes of divorce
to rediscover God's perfect plan for your life

"I would have despaired unless I had believed
that I would see the goodness of the LORD
In the land of the living."
Psalm 27:13, NASB

BARBARA KEISMAN

Contributing Authors

Tony Keisman

Denise Turner-Allen

Eilish Goodwin

All Scripture quotations, unless otherwise indicated, are taken from the HOLY BIBLE, New International Version®, NIV® Copyright © 1973, 1978, 1984, 2011 by Biblica, Inc.® Used by permission. All rights reserved worldwide.

Scripture taken from the NEW AMERICAN STANDARD BIBLE® (NASB), Copyright ©1960, 1962, 1963, 1968, 1971, 1972, 1973, 1975, 1977, 1995 by The Lockman Foundation. Used by permission.

Scripture taken from the New King James Version® (NKJV). Copyright © 1982 by Thomas Nelson. Used by permission. All rights reserved.

The ESV® Bible (The Holy Bible, English Standard Version®). ESV® Permanent Text Edition® (2016). Copyright © 2001 by Crossway, a publishing ministry of Good News Publishers. The ESV® text has been reproduced in cooperation with and by permission of Good News Publishers. All rights reserved.

Scripture quotations marked KJV are from The King James Version, Holy Bible. Public Domain.

We have chosen to capitalize all of the personal pronouns referring to God throughout our text, except when quoting from the NIV version of the Bible.

Copyright © 2017 Barbara Keisman
All rights reserved.
ISBN-13: 978-1545330289
ISBN-10: 154533028X

DEDICATION

This book is dedicated to my children – Sean, Stuart, and Carla – and to my family, the Bonner clan. You are all truly gifts from God to me. Your love and kindness carried me through my darkest times.

CONTENTS

"Never will I leave you; never will I forsake you."
Hebrews 13:5

"For I know the plans I have for you," declares the LORD, *"plans to prosper you and not to harm you, plans to give you hope and a future"*
Jeremiah 29:11

ACKNOWLEDGMENTS

A huge thanks goes to Janet Jackson for patiently editing change after change that I sent to her. I am grateful to have you in my life. And to the women who were willing to share their stories, I am blessed by your desire to help another person going through their midnight hour.

Chapter 1
Barbara's Story

Storms Will Come

"Therefore everyone who hears these words of mine and puts them into practice is like a wise man who built his house on the rock. The rain came down, the streams rose, and the winds blew and beat against that house; yet it did not fall, because it had its foundation on the rock. But everyone who hears these words of mine and does not put them into practice is like a foolish man who built his house on sand. The rain came down, the streams rose, and the winds blew and beat against that house, and it fell with a great crash." (Matthew 7:24-27)

In this Scripture, Jesus warns us to be careful about how we build our lives because storms would come to test whether we built our lives upon His words or with inferior materials. These storms can take on many different faces. Some storms can occur when a loved one dies, for another, it can happen when they receive the news of cancer. It can come through a job loss, a failed relationship, or a significant life disappointment that rocks your world. For me, it happened when my thirty-four-year marriage ended in divorce. My divorce threw me into a financial and emotional storm I had not prepared for.

My divorce didn't happen overnight, but after years of intercessory prayers asking the Lord to save it. Instead of my prayers being answered the way I had hoped for, everything precious to me that I had worked on for years was crashing before my eyes, and I felt helpless to stop this crash. But was I? The storm did come, but I could still choose to put God's Word into practice, trusting Him for an outcome that would glorify Him and save all that I held dear to my heart.

How we go through our storm will determine our outcome, just as much as how we built our lives, to begin with. These storms are only tests to see if we will continue to stand firm for the Lord during our times of adversity. By faith, we must keep our eyes focused on Jesus and His words, and not on the scary storm. We must put into practice all that we have learned prior to our time of testing if we are to come forth victorious.

My Story

On August 10, 1974, I married my high school sweetheart. I entered the marriage with dreams of having many exciting life adventures, holding hands with my new husband. However, that dream was short lived. Reality set in immediately as we had to deal with paying bills, leaving no money for fun. Life's pressures started there and never seemed to lift. Those pressures turned us against each other, and we started fighting.

Seven years into the marriage, our fighting had only increased and was wearing on me. I remembered looking in the mirror and was shocked to see how much I had aged in a few short years. I had done everything I could to try to fix our marriage, including going back to church. Even though I did experience some peace at church, it never seemed to change our lives. It was at that time that I met a Christian who shared her faith with me. I remember being very impressed as I listened to her talk about God and Jesus. It was like Jesus was her best friend who she talked to daily. She told me stories of miraculous answers to her prayers and those of other church members. It seemed to me that when she prayed, she actually believed God heard her prayers, whereas when I prayed, I merely hoped God heard my prayers.

After observing her for about six months, I decided that I needed what she had, and I asked Jesus to come into my life. I went home and asked my husband to do the same, and he agreed.

Did things between us get better? Yes and no. We did have a new rule book, the Bible, to help us make different decisions, but we still had our issues. Our hurts and patterns of behavior were still there. Even so, I experienced a feeling of peace I had been desperate for, and that peace kept me wanting more.

Shortly after our decision to invite Christ into our lives, we had our first child and decided that I should stay home to raise our children. Our lives were soon filled with raising our three children, work, and church. Throughout these years, the fighting continued. We had been pursuing and experiencing God's power in so many ways but had neglected to pursue His character with the same heartfelt energy. We had the conviction of the Holy Spirit, but we did not obey His convictions enough to experience the change needed to bring us peace. God never quit on us though, and I kept going forward, trusting that He would heal our marriage and our character flaws in His time.

Time went on, and the fighting never ended. The hurts compiled and my hopes for Jesus to heal our marriage seemed unattainable, considering we had continued to fight every year since we had accepted Jesus into our lives. With each year, I became increasingly angrier, and so did Tony. The Bible says a house divided will fall, and after 34 years of marriage, Tony filed for divorce.

We had decided not to hire an attorney and to work things out between ourselves. Thirty days after filing, we were to appear in court for what I thought was a pre-divorce hearing. The judge sent us into a room to divide up our marital property, and half an hour later, we were standing in front of the judge divorced. I ran out of that courtroom sobbing because I had no idea that I would be divorced that day. It was the worst day of my life!

We went home, and a few hours later, our daughter and one of our sons walked in with flowers to give me. Still crying, I told them I was so sorry for having failed them. My daughter stopped me, and emphatically said that I had never failed them. Her words of love instantly removed the shame that had come upon me. Next, they went to find their father and hugged him. God's undeserved grace and love flowed through them to us at that moment and has never stopped.

Overnight Money Concerns

It wasn't long after our divorce that the financial reality of our divorce set in, as Tony had been the primary breadwinner in our home. A few years before our divorce, we had decided to close our photography store so I could devote more time to writing. I had taken a part-time job as a school bus driver to supplement our income while writing. So, when the divorce happened, that was my only income.

The first year of our divorce, I worked to eliminate every bill that I could live without. Even so, I didn't know how I would ever be able to continue to pay the mortgage and all the other remaining bills with a part-time bus driver's paycheck combined with Tony's alimony check, which was scheduled to end in five years.

The more I thought about it, the more fear overcame me. Then, I remember getting angry and saying in my heart and maybe even out loud, "Devil, you are trying to make me afraid that I won't be able to make it without Tony's income, so I'm going to make you regret that you made me afraid, and I am going to give God a $200 offering." That moment changed everything. With that statement and commitment to give! I immediately knew how I was going to make it financially. I had learned a few things in the 27 years I had been a Christian, and the one thing I knew for sure was that I could never out-give God. I knew that the only way to fight my financial fears was to place my complete trust in God, and my offering did just that. I was fighting fire with fire. Faith rose up, and fear had to flee.

Forewarned

Two years before we were divorced, the Lord gave me a

powerful warning to get debt free. I can't remember how I received this communication, but I do remember how God confirmed it. Tony and I were in the car discussing the Lord's instructions to become debt free. I said, "Tony, this word from the Lord to get debt free is very strong." Just as I said those words, I noticed the license plate of the car in front of us. It read "forewarned." When I saw it, I pointed it out and said, "Tony, I don't know what is coming our way, but if we don't get debt free, God says it is on us. He tried to warn us." At the time, we had a large amount of credit card debt, and because of this warning, we decided to refinance our house and pay off our credit cards. Two years later, when we were divorced, I understood why the Lord had led us to do that. Had we not listened to God's communication to get debt free, I could have never kept the house, which I would need to do what God had planned for me in the future.

Rejection and Loneliness

Soon after the divorce, I remember the Holy Spirit communicating to me that He hadn't divorced me. His communication of love gave me the faith to believe that, despite my many failures, He would be there for me whenever I needed Him. He also warned me not to make potentially harmful choices due to feelings of rejection and abandonment. I wasn't to run towards other men to prove I was still desirable or valued, but to trust Him instead to meet those emotional needs. In the eleven years since my divorce, I have never felt it was God's will for me to date. I'm not saying I didn't try to date, but I never felt it was God's will. So, I would always decline. I soon realized that He wanted me to take this time to heal my soul and pursue His will for my life. I was to look to Jesus as my husband, knowing I could turn to Him whenever I needed His provision, protection, or emotional support.

Even with the Lord's assurances, I would find myself slipping into depression due to loneliness, especially during the weekends when I had more free time. I often asked God to fill this emptiness, and God always made a way. I am so grateful to my children, family, and friends for including me in their lives after my divorce. Their kind attentions kept me safe from the despair that loneliness can bring.

Jealousy and Bitterness

I had decided from day one of our divorce that I would never exclude Tony from any of our family events. This meant that we would see each other quite often. During these outings, he would tell us what he had been doing and buying. It was hard to hear about how well he was doing when I was struggling. I had to choose to be silent (hard for me) and resist the temptation to spend money I didn't have, just to satisfy my emotional needs. I had learned years earlier not to use a credit card for my personal spending because I knew from past experience that it would only make matters worse. If I couldn't pay cash, I did without.

With all the loss I was experiencing, I found feelings of bitterness rising up in me towards Tony. It was hard to see him enjoying his life when I was not. I had to reason with myself that the Lord could satisfy me despite my new financial or social status. In honesty, this stretched my faith, but in my heart, I knew how spiritually dangerous bitterness could be.

I discovered that when I focused on Tony instead of God, it kept me feeling bitter. To fight this bitterness, I had to admit that I was bitter and take my focus off Tony. By faith, I chose to believe that God was in control and had good things planned for me. I chose to believe that my best years were still ahead.

Keeping the House

In the divorce decree, I had asked for enough alimony to cover me for the first year, figuring I could find a way to get by with less during the next four years of remaining alimony. The loan on our house was underwater after the housing crash, so there was no possibility of selling it. Not feeling led to move, I asked Tony if I could keep the house, thinking I would never be able to afford to buy another house with my income, and he agreed. With that decision, we both wondered how I would be able to afford to pay the mortgage, but I had faith I could do it with God's help. Strangely enough, I didn't feel like I was supposed to look for a second job to make more money. I knew it would be all God or I was in trouble. It was not long before I needed His miraculous provision.

Lost Health Insurance

Nine months after our divorce, the trauma of it had overtaken my emotions, and I could not stop thinking about it and all the years of fighting before it. Bad memories started to torment my mind 24/7, and I asked the Lord to remove those memories and the increasing anger from my heart. This is what happened next...

I was riding my bicycle along the lakefront on a beautiful Saturday morning reliving all the hurts of the past when I came upon some old broken-down railroad tracks. My tires slipped in-between two of the tracks throwing my bike to the ground and me with it. Instinctively, I threw my right hand out to stop my fall.

After the fall, I lay on the pavement for a moment to see what injuries I had experienced. Not feeling any pain, I noticed that my right wrist area had a significant bump on it. I could tell I had hurt it, but it didn't really hurt. I called for help using my cell phone and immediately went to have x-rays taken. Wondering how long it would take to know the results of the x-rays, I walked up to the reception desk where two nurses were sitting and talking. As I approached them, they stopped talking and said, "We were just talking about you. We saw your x-rays and can't figure out why you're laughing. You have a very bad break." Laughing, I said, "That's true, but I am not in pain." God's grace was once again very present in my day of trouble.

The doctor sent me to see a bone specialist who diagnosed surgery. I asked him if I could have the weekend to pray about it before I committed to having the surgery. Throughout our years as Christians, our family sought to heal through prayer alone, and only when we felt led to go to a doctor, did we go. Going to a doctor to be treated was never our first response. I needed time to ask God if He wanted to heal me miraculously or through a doctor. Both would require a miracle because I had lost my health insurance through the divorce and had not been able to afford it on my bus driver's income.

During that time of prayer, I asked God why He had allowed me to break my wrist. I felt like I had just been disciplined, and my feelings were hurt. I turned on a Christian TV channel and started to watch the woman speaking. As she spoke, she turned to the camera and lifted her arm in the air grabbing her wrist with her other hand saying, "What you are going through is to cause you to cling to the Lord." She was holding her wrist exactly where mine was broken, and I knew I had heard from the Lord.

After prayer, I felt led to go ahead with the surgery. Now I had to figure out how to pay for it. I called the hospital, and they informed me that the operation would cost $25,000, and I couldn't schedule it without a $12,000 down payment. I didn't have a dime in the bank, so this wasn't an option. The bone specialist had told me about a cheaper outpatient surgery he knew of, so I called to find out about this option. For some strange reason, no one returned my phone call. It had now been three days since my accident. As I was trying to figure out what to do, my sister called, and I told her what I was going through. I said to her, "I don't know what to do, I have no experience with hospitals or doctors, and I can't even get them to tell me how much this is going to cost." She said, "Barb, don't worry about this. I'll take care of it."

And she did.

The morning before our conversation, I had been praying when I was given a vision of my very large family coming to my rescue. In the vision, I felt liquid love come over me as I envisioned them circled around me, and I began sobbing with gratitude for their whole-hearted love and concern for me. All my feelings of loneliness and weakness lifted from me as I experienced their love through this vision. Then it happened. My sister called me two hours later to tell me that surgery had been scheduled and had been paid for by my family. She continued by saying that I wasn't to worry about paying them back. I love my family for so many reasons, and one of them is their generosity. I could not have been prouder of them at that moment.

Due to my wrist, I would also be out of work for a month and I wondered how the Lord was going to provide. Without saying a word to anyone about my need, my father sent me a check for $5,000 to cover my bills until I could work again. I was "blessed beyond blessed" by the love of my family during this time, and it began the healing process I needed to go through.

That same year, my daughter left to go on a six-month mission trip and both my sons were married to amazing women. I could not help wondering why my children had so little fear of marriage after witnessing their parents' marriage end so badly. However, this was another example of God's grace. Around two years later, my daughter also met and married a wonderful man and God's grace continued to follow our family.

Revisiting Old Dreams

Our children were all over 18 years of age when we divorced, so within a few short years, I went from a full to an empty house. My life had been focused on taking care of my family, so I didn't know how I would survive emotionally without them. I remember asking the Lord to replace all the loss I was experiencing, and He did. During the first two years, I joined a board to raise funds to bring the Boys and Girls Club to our city. Joining this cause gave me a chance to meet new people and to get my mind off my problems. We were able to open the club two years later. It was then that the Lord spoke to me about my dream of creating a women's fashion line for charity, and I couldn't have been poorer at that time.

Twenty-six years earlier, I had tried to start this dream when my children were still toddlers. I could see then that this dream was going to require more time and money than I had to give if I was going to be the mom I needed to be. So, after praying about it, the Lord impressed upon me to put my dream on hold and that it would happen later in life. Now it seemed that time had arrived. I had much time on my hands, and I needed a cause to live for now that my children were grown and on their own.

The earthquake in Haiti had occurred around this time and I remember wanting to donate towards helping the victims in Haiti but had little money to give. While thinking about the little I did have, I was given a vision of a woman from Haiti asking me why I had not cared enough about her to help. When she asked me that question, I defensively thought about my own financial difficulties. Countering that defense, another thought came to my mind that made my previous defense seem wrong. The fact was that I lived in America where the possibilities of creating wealth were mine if I chose to go for it. The woman in my vision didn't have that option. Feelings of shame overcame me for thinking only of my own needs and for not wanting to complicate my life with difficulties so I could help her. In my heart, I knew I had to follow my dream and I decided to go forward, trusting God to help me in this cause.

I have a background in fashion, as a print model in my early twenties, and later as a fashion photographer. However, it had been years since I had even looked at a fashion magazine, so I felt clueless as to what the current fashion trends were. I did know how to sew, but I had no formal training in clothing design. With the knowledge I did possess, I knew I would have to find fabric resources, learn how to make patterns, buy machines, connect with women to help me sew the clothing, and then find ways to sell it. The enormity of it all seemed overwhelming. Even so, all things are possible with God, and I went forward with faith, believing that each of these concerns would somehow be resolved.

Do Not Despise the Day of Small Beginnings

I started where I was. I needed to find affordable fabric to practice on, so I began by buying existing tees and redesigning them. Because I was unable to find the tees

I wanted, I went to Walmart and bought men's 100 percent cotton tees, re-cut them, and turned them into really cute women's tees. I listed them on Etsy, and they sold. Even though I was experiencing some success, I also experienced a host of other emotions as I tried to figure out how to go forward without the needed experience that brings knowledge. It was not long before I realized how hard it would be to birth this dream of mine. When I would get discouraged, the Lord would ask me, "Is there not a cause worth fighting for?"

If I had to describe these beginning years, it was like I had been put into a dark room, and to avoid being hurt, I had my hands reaching out in front of me searching for the light switch. I decided to go on a fast to seek God for wisdom, and afterward, the Lord shed some light on my path. He told me that my fashions would be involved with the city of Chicago, and to keep my eyes open for such an opportunity.

Two weeks after this fast, I heard about a fashion competition that the city of Chicago was hosting, and I entered it. I was one of twenty-six designers, chosen to participate in an education program, along with the opportunity to sell my fashions at a pop-up shop close to Magnificent Mile during the Christmas season.

It was through this competition that I made valuable connections in the fashion industry. As I talked to the other 26 designers, I learned how they found their customers, where they bought fabric, and received answers to many other questions I had had. Soon I was spending thousands of dollars each year to produce my clothing line, hoping and praying that I would make my money back. Each year, with God's help, I did just that.

Alimony Ends

A year after I started my fashion line, the Lord impressed upon me to stop taking alimony from my ex-husband and to trust Him instead for my provision. To help me in this transition, I had been listening to Mike Bickle's 19-hour teaching on the Song of Songs. His teaching transformed my thinking. What a love story between God and man! As I listened to it, I felt loved and protected by a God who I came to know as the lover of my soul. An intimacy was forming between God and me, and He wanted that intimacy to grow through trust. I did as He had led me and told Tony that I would no longer need his alimony.

To Tony's credit, a year after I ended our alimony arrangement, he walked into my house and handed me keys to a brand-new car. When I realized what he had done, my first reaction was to decline his very generous gift, but I could tell he was giving me this gift from his heart. I gratefully accepted it. His heart-felt gift played a tremendous part in healing more of my past hurts. There was a small car payment that I insisted on taking over, believing I could somehow pay it. I was grateful to Tony, and to God, for providing a dependable car that I would not have to worry about making repairs on.

Throughout those first years after our divorce, I never missed a payment on anything, nor did I feel it necessary to get a second job to pay the bills, other than my new fashion business. I did feel led to rent out a room in my house, and that money paid my utilities and gave me some much-needed fellowship. I lived a frugal life, content with what the Lord provided for me. I even prospered somewhat during those years and was able to make some improvements to my house, and thanks to the generosity of my son and his wife, I attended a niece's wedding in Cancun. Then in 2014, I hit another wall that almost did me in.

Business Woes

Almost all retail profits are made in the last quarter of every year. The Christmas season is critical to making a profit, and that's when I hit this wall. It was the end of October, and I had scheduled three end-of-the-year shows to sell my clothing when it felt like something had punched me in the stomach. Three days later, my condition had grown worse, and my children became very concerned. They started talking to me about going to a doctor, but since I didn't have insurance, I wanted to see if I would get better without a doctor's care. I soon became convinced that I would need at least an antibiotic, so I agreed to go to the ER. Through a series of tests, the hospital discovered that my appendix had burst, and off I went to have emergency surgery.

Just before going into surgery, the surgeon said to me, "You only had 48 hours left to live before you came to the hospital." God had given me such peace, and I thought to myself, "God would never have let that happen." After the surgery, the following Scripture came to me during my morning devotions, *"Though I walk through the valley of the shadow of death, I shall fear no evil for you art with me."* (Psalm 23:4)

After the surgery, my family and Tony came to help me during my recovery time. Romans 8:28 says, *"And we know that in all things God works for the good of those who love him, who have been called according to his purpose."* God will turn every event in our lives out for good, and that happened when Tony came to help me during my time of need. His act of love and concern for me healed more of my hurts, and a deeper level of forgiveness took place between us.

Due to my illness, I lost the sales from two of the shows I had scheduled, but I still had one larger holiday show to make the money I needed to pay off my credit cards. Making a profit was no longer a thought. Even though that show brought in huge sales, I was left with a $17,000 credit card debt, which would have to be carried over into the next year.

My business credit card debt, combined with my new hospital debt, added up to around $100,000 of accumulated debt in one year. I had just turned 60 years of age, and I was painfully aware that this was no time in life to be in debt. I was beginning to feel like God had failed me.

Discouragement set in, and I desperately wanted to quit my dream. I had worked two jobs (my bus driving and clothing company) for four years and had nothing to show for it. I had also been telling my customers that I was going to give 10 percent of all the sales from my fashions to Haiti, and I needed to keep my word (which I did). My world got darker and darker with depression and discouragement. And God kept asking me, "Is there not a cause worth fighting for?" All I can say is that I would have quit had I not been in debt. My debt kept me going. I secretly thought that I would work for another year to pay my debt off and then quit. However, God kept asking me the same question over and over again, "Is there not a cause?"

Here's what God did within one year. The hospital asked me to apply for charity, which I did. Charity covered most of my bills leaving me about $6,000 to pay, which I figured would be a reasonable co-patient portion of the bill if I had had insurance. At the end of the 2015 year, due to record sales, I was able to pay off two years of business credit card debt, and even buy some furniture for my living room and kitchen. That year, I was never late on a payment for anything. To God be all the glory for the great things He has done!

Time to Reflect

I recently started thinking about the eleven years I have been divorced, and all the Lord has done for me. During the first year of my divorce, my daughter gave me a prophetic word that said my divorce would launch me into my future. When she gave me that word, I couldn't figure out how it could be true. But the truth is, I would never have started my fashion line if I had been married. I would have been too afraid to spend the money I needed to for fear of adding more stress to my already stressed-out marriage. Even though it would have been great to have had the financial support of a husband, in the end, it was easier for me to start my dream trusting only in the Lord's help.

The divorce also revealed my hidden fears. We can say we trust the Lord, but then we do everything we can so that we won't have to trust Him or anyone else for that matter. One of my hidden fears was thinking I couldn't make it financially without Tony's assistance. To help me fight this fear, the Lord gave my daughter another prophetic word for me. She created and gave me a card that said: "God will make a way." That message has proven true over and over again. No matter what came my way, the Lord always made a way. I stand stronger and more secure today because I refused to run toward another man for help in my time of need. I still have that card taped to my bedroom door.

Last year, I was able to afford a Christian medical sharing plan that met the Affordable Care Act requirements. I must say that even though I could not afford health insurance for many years, I did what was necessary to maintain good health. I eat those recommended five to seven servings of fruits and veggies, minimized my meat consumption and sweets, replaced sugar with stevia, drank beverages like water, green tea, and smoothies made with fruit and spinach, exercised, took whole food vitamins and supplements, etc. I believe God created food to keep our bodies healthy, and I did my best to eat those foods regularly. We can all participate in preventative healthcare, which in the end, will be far cheaper than getting sick. If I ever have to choose again between spending money on health insurance or on healthy foods, I will always choose healthy foods. Now I can afford both.

During those eleven years, God continually gave me the grace and faith to pay my tithe and offerings. That was a miracle because I cannot tell you how I was able to pay all of my living expenses and then be able to give too. Admittedly, living a very frugal life and juggling many things to stay on top of my bills got hard. But month after month, God's faithfulness never failed me.

The bottom line is that my divorce caused me to experience God's faithfulness and great love towards me. It caused me to discover more of my God-given gifts and find the future God had planned for me all along. Although I did not want to be divorced, and it's never God's perfect will for any marriage to end in divorce, I now know He can still bring forth His will though divorced men and women who will humbly lay down their lives and commit to obeying His Word.

The Greatest Blessing

God's greatest blessing given to me during the past eleven years was seen in my family. God not only preserved my family unit, but He also increased our love for each other. Throughout our divorce, Tony and I worked through many difficult emotions to maintain our family, and it paid off. Today our family is a loving, supportive, and growing family unit with seven amazing grandchildren to enjoy. Unfortunately, the issues between Tony and I still exist. We may no longer be husband and wife, but after 45 years of being in each other's lives, we are still family.

Chapter 2
Tony's Story

As I write this chapter, it has been eleven years since I asked Barbara for a divorce, a divorce I never wanted. Writing this story is by far, one of the hardest things I have ever done. But Barb asked me to write it, and I also felt it was the Lord's will. Since the divorce, Barbara and I have made peace by working through so many difficult conversations, and we both felt my story could help another man avoid some of the many mistakes I made in our marriage and perhaps help them have hope that the decisions they make today will bring them into a better future.

Where do I begin? I met and fell head over heels in love with Barbara when we were both just 16 years old and attending the same high school. I had known her brother because we were both football players. From the time we met, we dated exclusively throughout high school. After graduation, I signed up to go away to attend a technical school for electronics for two years, while Barb attended a local community college. The commute between us was tough, and a year later, we decided to marry even though I had one more year to finish my education.

That first year of marriage was hard. I had to work full time and go to school, and Barb eventually found a nighttime position at a fast-food restaurant. We had no friends and no money. We both looked forward to the day I would graduate and get a good-paying job. I did graduate but was very disappointed with the first two jobs I worked as a technician. I hated these low paying jobs and became frustrated, thinking I would be stuck working them with little possibility for professional growth or increased income.

It was around this time that Barb started to model in Cleveland where some of the department stores picked her up and used her for their newspaper advertisements. This was exciting for Barbara, but she knew she had a limited clientele living in Cleveland and wondered how she would do in a larger market.

Desperate for friends and family, we decided to move back to our hometown, where I decided to start selling cars for a local car dealer. I was not good at this and was soon let go. After taking another terrible job out of desperation, I landed a job with Ford Motor Company working on the assembly line. The work was hard, and the hours were long, but the money was good. When I started the job, I told myself this was just for a couple of years. I didn't want to go back to college to finish a 4-year degree believing I would find a better job eventually.

Barb had gone to Chicago to see what modeling in a broader market would be like and found out that it was not going to be an easy transition. She returned to Ohio and started working at the Ford plant with me. We worked long hours but made great money, and within a short period of time, we purchased our first income property thinking we would buy more in the future. But as it turned out, the recession hit, and we were both looking at being laid off.

I had recently purchased my first 35mm camera and found that I loved being a photographer. I studied photography and took pictures of everything, then printed them in my darkroom. Barbara could see I had a talent for this, and she suggested that we both move to Chicago to pursue modeling and photography careers. I didn't see much future staying and waiting to be hired back to a job working on the assembly line, so we moved to Chicago.

Photography Position

I quickly secured an assistant photographer position with a well-known freelance product/food photographer. This position didn't pay much, but it was the gateway to professional photography. Overnight I was immersed in an industry that only a few people experience. I met so many interesting and talented people and saw how they conducted business. The money that a top commercial photographer could make was amazing. Even though my job required that I work 60 to 80 hours a week at minimum wage, I felt that it was worth it if I could use this as a stepping stone to becoming a freelance photographer. This put a huge strain on my marriage as it left Barbara completely alone. She would complain, but I didn't see any way to make her happy and my boss too. So, I did what I thought I had to do telling myself that it would all be worth it. I had no idea how much damage I was doing to my relationship with my wife.

Barbara got into modeling at the age of 21, which was fairly late to start a modeling career, and now she was competing with many younger models. She had learned the business and knew that new girls needed to have their photos taken before a modeling agency would consider them. So, she decided to be a photographer and started to shoot model composites. In a very short time, she was making enough money to allow me to leave my job and join her in our first attempt to have a business together. Working together was difficult, but our combined talents made it possible to make enough money to pay the bills and try to figure out what was next.

The stress of working together combined with financial difficulties continued to increase until neither of us knew if we could continue in our marriage for much longer. It was at this time we met a Christian model who led Barbara to the Lord. Afterward, Barbara came home and asked me to join her in her decision to become a Christian.

Seven years before this, I had prayed and asked Jesus into my life when I was going to the tech school before we were married. When I shared this with Barbara, she was not ready to do the same, so I backed off and did not commit to living as a Christian. Now God had made it come full circle. I agreed, knowing it was the right thing to do. I wish I could say that our problems and the fighting ended there, but they did not. I was so frustrated with my life that I would punch holes through walls and scream terrible things at my wife. Her anger led to retaliation, and she would scream back at me with equally hurtful words.

New Family Pressures

Despite all the problems, we kept trying to go forward and make a life together. By now, we had been married for almost seven years. Soon after our decision to become Christians, God blessed us with our first son. This was the highlight of my married life so far. Unfortunately, I also experienced more anxieties as I realized I was responsible for caring for my growing family. We had done well enough in our business to move to a very nice expensive, loft/studio in the near north area of Chicago.

After our son was born, we started to try to make the transition to commercial product photography. This was very difficult, and I was unable to get enough work to pay for our new loft. My anxieties increased, and I lashed out at Barbara over and over again until I came to my breaking point. This happened after we became six months behind on paying our studio rent. Our landlord had shown us kindness and never threatened to evict us. Not wanting to take advantage of his kindness or to accumulate any more back rent, we decided to move out of the loft, and I sent Barbara, who was pregnant with our second child, back to Ohio to live with her parents while I stayed and worked a part-time job at a large hospital.

I worked nights at the hospital and as a freelance photography assistant during the day. By doing this, I was able to make enough money to rent a small cottage on the south side of the city and move my family back to Chicago. While working at that hospital, I saw so many hurting people, and it made me realize how blessed I was.

We moved into the cottage two months before my second son was born. He came about two weeks before Christmas. I was happy to have my family back, but the hospital job had ended. I prayed and asked God what I should do to make an income. The small church we had been attending needed a lot of work and my Pastor asked me if I could do some of the needed repairs. I agreed to do the work, and I decided not to worry about how I would pay our bills. I told Barbara that I was going to work for the church to build walls and do any other work they needed to be done and trust God to provide for us until the work started up again.

God Gives Us a Huge Deliverance

It was a month and a half before I got a job offer to do some catalog product photography. This small job turned into a large job that kept me busy for the next four weeks. With the money from this job, we were able to pay off our back rent with money left over to live on. This experience was a great morale booster for my faith in God, and my hope that I was finally going to be able to make it as a photographer and provide for my family. Soon we would have our third child, a daughter.

The church we attended on the south side of Chicago was located across the street from an intercity housing project. My wife and I got involved in children's ministry in our church. There were many kids with single parents that needed love and attention. They were tough but responded well to the message of love and hope that the Bible teaches. The church family became our extended family, and our kids grew up going to church every Wednesday night and Sunday morning and evening. We also got involved in street ministry in our neighborhood and downtown Chicago in the well-known Rush Street area. We would sing contemporary Christian songs over a portable sound system and told people about the great things God was doing in our lives and how He could do the same for them.

Because I did not want to raise my kids in the city, I started praying and looking for a way to move to a suburb of Chicago. At this point, I had enough experience to get a job working as a corporate photographer if I could find the right company. I heard through a friend that a job was open at a large medical supply company in the northern suburbs. I applied and was hired as the Senior Photographer in charge of the photography department. What a blessing this was! I had finally gotten a job that would pay me a decent salary and gave me professional satisfaction.

One year later, the Lord led us to move closer to that job through a prophetic word. We moved to a city 50 miles north of Chicago where we bought a home and raised our kids.

My Corporate Photography Position Ends

Life was good. I finally had a corporate photography job, and I thought that this job with its prestige and pay would bring me some satisfaction and give us peace.

Four years after I had been hired, the company informed me that they were closing down the photography, graphics, and video departments and instructed me to sell off all the studio equipment. What a blow this was!

God Gives Barbara a Divine Dream

Just before all of this happened, Barbara told me of a dream she had. In the dream, we were walking down a path when we came upon an expensive Hasselblad camera someone had thrown out and she told me to pick it up, which I did. We went a little further and found another Hasselblad camera and I picked that one up too. When she told me this dream, I told her that no one ever throws these cameras out. She told me that maybe someone would sell them so cheap it would be like they were throwing them out and to keep my eyes open for them.

As I went through all the equipment and started putting together how much it was worth, I decided to put together an offer to buy everything with the financial help of another photographer I had met. I showed him the deal I had in mind, and he agreed to become a partner, and we purchased all the equipment with the intent of forming a business as a team. Within the purchase was three Hasselblad cameras. One of them was used exclusively with a digital camera back. We sold off the equipment we didn't want and that paid for the equipment we did keep. Barbara and I ended up keeping the other two Hasselblad cameras to use for wedding photography. God works in mysterious ways.

The photography world was going digital. One of the most important items purchased in the deal was a top of the line digital camera that was to be used to do catalog photography. My new partner and I set up shop in the basement of his house and we worked together trying to sell the new digital photography service we had purchased. We worked hard to make our product excellent and everyone we worked for loved the results. The problem was the technology was so new, and many clients had already made contracts with printers and separators who used film-based photography. Convincing them to switch to this new system was almost impossible.

My Partner Shuts Me Out

Then one day, I went to my partner's house and he refused to let me in and have access to the digital camera and computer equipment. I never saw this coming. It created huge anxieties in me, as overnight I was out of a job. This shut out continued for six months. Eventually, we hired a lawyer and were able to reach a buyout settlement for my part of the business. This was one of the most stressful years of my life.

Just before the shut out started, Barbara had received a word from the Lord to open up a one-hour photo lab, and through a series of financial miracles, we were able to purchase an entire lab and secure a storefront for under $10,000. This store also served as a photography studio for her, and the lab would provide her with quality inexpensive prints to sell to her clients. It was God's mercy that this store had been set up just before my partner had shut me out. I changed directions again and put all my energy into the one-hour photography store we had opened.

Within three years, I had lost a corporate position, with all its benefits, had a business stolen from me from someone I had trusted and was thrown back into the insecurities of self-employment. I had never even worked at a lab before we purchased ours. Overnight, I had to learn how to make it all work, adding more stress to my life. I would spend many hours cleaning, repairing, and changing chemicals that were used to process film and make color prints. In between all this, I did some freelance photography work when I got the chance.

For four years, our income came from the combined one-hour lab and photography. Then Barbara felt led to quit her photography career to devote more time to writing. She asked me if I wanted to take over the lab, but I didn't see a future for it mostly because we could not compete with the large box stores who were processing film practically giving away the printing. Additionally, our equipment was old and in constant need of repair, and we couldn't afford to buy expensive new digital equipment that was needed if we were going to stay in this business. We closed the store and Barbara took on a part-time position as a school bus driver to supplement our income.

While we had that business, I never believed I could afford to quit even though I felt like I was drowning and over my head in deep water. Barbara and I disagreed on almost everything concerning the business. We were always at odds fighting with one another. I wondered what would happen next, and I looked for any way to escape having to deal with all of this.

My Mid-life Crisis

My 50th birthday had come and gone. It was around this time that I hit what many people call a mid-life crisis. I was emotionally and physically tired of all the struggle and the fact I didn't seem to be getting anywhere. I felt like a complete failure as a husband and father. My body was starting to show signs of aging. At the age of 35, I had been diagnosed with degenerative arthritis in my left hip. I was told that I would eventually need a hip replacement. My hip had been getting worse with each year, and I was in pain constantly.

I knew that my daughter would be getting married someday and I wondered how I would pay for her wedding or my needed hip surgery without a good-paying job or health insurance. I felt like I wanted to explode most of the time, and I looked for a way to escape.

I have always owned a motorcycle, and before we had children, Barb and I would go on rides to escape the city on weekends. It was a cheap getaway we both loved doing. Remembering my love of riding, I turned to motorcycles again for my escape. It started with a friend I met in my new church. I bought a bike from him that had major problems and I put it back together. This became my escape machine. I used it to run away whenever I could getaway. Barbara also loved riding behind me. Then one day, I decided to buy a new motorcycle after I got the settlement from my business. It was a single-seat sport bike. This made my wife very angry. Now I was cutting her out of the picture. I still had the other motorcycle, but the mold had been cast. I had planted the wrong seed in her mind, and it was growing.

Friends and Motorcycle Riding

I was sitting in the parking lot of an electronics store on the single-seat motorcycle I had bought when a young guy drove up in a little black S10 pickup truck and stuck his head out the window and asked me about the bike. It turned out that he had wanted to buy it, but I had beaten him to it. We became best friends. I had not had a best friend since high school. I never got very close to any of the guys I met in church or in the photo business. Best friends are special and only come along a few times in your life. It turned out that we had quite a bit in common. Our friendship grew, and so did my time away from my family. My friend loved motorcycles as much or more than I, and he introduced me to many new people that liked to ride. I became a member of a motorcycle group and went on rides and attended rallies regularly. This was my escape. Unfortunately, I did not understand how much damage I was doing to my relationship.

My friend worked for one of the largest electronics manufacturers in the world, and he called one day to tell me that his boss was looking to fill some technician openings. I was hesitant since I had been away from the field of electronics for so many years, but I had much experience troubleshooting our lab equipment, and I had developed skills on the computer using digital photography. I got an interview and took the required tests to show my knowledge of electronics. His boss liked me, and I got the job.

We Divorce

The job was a night shift position that required three 12-hour shifts starting on Saturday afternoon. The job provided a good income and benefits, but it took me away from my family on weekends and strained my relationship with Barbara even more. Even though I had much free time during the week, I divided that time between her and my friends and Barbara felt she was getting the short end of my time. The strain on our relationship had taken its toll, and we were never able to recover. I had lost my will to work on my relationship to make it better. Even when I tried, I would fail and usually make things worse. It was too little, too late. I didn't want to be free to pursue another woman or lifestyle. I just wanted to be free from a bad marriage. I felt like I would never be able to make things right. It was too difficult to face and try to fix the problems that had taken years to create. I eventually told Barbara I wanted a divorce. Soon after this, we filed for divorce, and in about a month, it was final. I moved out of our home and went to live with a friend who lived a couple of miles away.

I continued to work as a technician, and during this time, two significant events took place in my life. My daughter met the man she would marry, and I had the surgery to replace my bad hip. Through my new job, I realized how God had provided for my previous concerns once again.

Nine years later, the company I worked for was sold and my team was laid off. I decided to retire early because I did not have the desire to find another job. I decided I would continue to do some freelance photo work to supplement my income. I had hoped that after the divorce, Barbara and I would be able to find a way to reconcile our differences and maybe in time get remarried.

Things did not go the way I had hoped, and even though we were able to share our family events, there was a lot of tension and unresolved problems between us. After a while, I thought it would be better to get away from the area and try to make a new start. I purchased an RV and decided to move to Tennessee. I tried to make the transition, but it seemed like God had other plans for me.

In 2014 Barbara had emergency surgery for a burst appendix. I realized that this could have caused her death. I felt guilty because she was alone, and I realized I still loved her and did not want to lose her. I knew in my heart I needed to help while she recovered. I returned and stayed with her for the next month to help in her recovery. This also started our relationship's healing process but also revealed that we still had our issues between us. So, after she recovered, I returned to Tennessee, where I continued my search for a new life.

A year later, my oldest son's wife gave birth to their second son. Doctors found that he had a major heart defect and he was rushed into surgery two days after he was born. He would need two more surgeries to correct the problem, and this required a lot of hospital visits and time away from home for his parents. I offered to move in and live with them to help watch their other son. I left Tennessee and moved all my belonging back to Illinois. I knew this was the right thing to do. It also helped heal some of the wounds I had created in my family due to the divorce.

Dating

When people get divorced, they usually move on and find someone else. I had thought about dating, but I dismissed it as a bad idea. Then, my friend introduced me to a woman that I decided to date. It became clear to me after a short time that we were not a good match and I decided to stop seeing her. It was a painful but necessary lesson I had to learn. I have decided to stay single for the rest of my life. I found that I did not want to complicate my life with another relationship. I love my kids, and seven grandkids, and I know Barbara does too. We are both thankful for the good things God has allowed us to have despite our problems.

Currently, I am assisting my aging father. I am the oldest of five children, retired and single, which made me the best person to do this. I am enjoying getting to spend time with my father again, even with the new constraints it has brought to my life.

This brings us to today. We have a loving and supportive family, and I am so grateful that God preserved the best thing in my life. Grace was given to us, and it produced love and commitment to overlook our offenses.

The following are some of the things I discovered about myself and what I think I could have done differently. I am hoping these hard-learned lessons will help another man in crisis.

I have discovered that:

1) Relationships are strengthened when you are willing to lay down your life to serve those you love. Selfish living destroys relationships.

2) Priorities are essential to living a successful life. I wrongly prioritized my life with my goals in mind thinking my relationships could be ignored until I had achieved some of my other desires. I have since learned to put God first, family second, job third, and friends and hobbies last.

3) That harsh words can linger in a person's memory for a lifetime and can destroy their spirit. To undo the damage your words produced in them, you will have to replace them with 10 times more words of affirmation and acts of love.

4) That uncontrolled anger destroys relationships and causes people to distrust you. I was just trying to release the stress in my life and didn't think my frustrations would hurt the people

around me.

5) Rather than overload your wife with your stresses, seek out another man, who you respect and is spiritually mature to talk to or go to a therapist. You do need to talk things out, and you need an objective person to give you the needed feedback to change your life.

6) Realize that hard times come to all people, and God uses them to better prepare you for His plan. They were never meant to destroy you.

7) God never quits on you. Instead, He continuously reroutes a person going in the wrong direction to bring them back into His will and plan for their life. So, don't ever quit on Him or yourself.

Chapter 3
Death of a Dream

Most of us get married with a dream in mind. We fantasize about what our perfect life would look like married to the person of our dreams. Maybe it was a house on the lake with three kids, a good-paying corporate job, fun-filled vacations, then on to your retirement years travailing the world and growing old with the love of your life. We all enter marriage wearing rose colored glasses. Protecting our dreams, we ignore the failed marriages surrounding us, believing that what happened to them won't happen to us. And then it does.

Your perfect marriage slowly eroded when life got harder, and those hardships brought out the worse in you and your spouse. In time, you only see destruction and pain as you find you have been unable to fix your marriage and now it has failed from years of ill-spoken words or selfish acts just wanting to get your needs met at the sake of your spouse's needs. What happened to the man or woman of your dreams? How did they become so indifferent and even hurtful? Left unchanged, hurts and patterns of bad behavior start to pile up until all you can dream about is being freed from the horribleness of your marriage.

This scenario has left me to wonder how feelings of love could turn into hate in seemingly so short a time. But it can, and it does. And afterward, you are left wondering if your dream marriage could ever happen again or if you lost your only chance at love.

I feel for the spouse who never saw their divorce coming. They knew that life had gotten busy, and the connection between their spouse and themselves had waned, but they had no idea that their partner in life had emotionally checked out of their marriage long ago and was secretly planning their escape. The shock of their spouse's betrayal followed by a fast divorce launched them on an emotional roller coaster with no end in sight. Afterward, they look back searching for any clues they missed that could have warned them that their marriage had been hanging on the edge of a cliff just waiting to crash.

Self-doubts and trust issues cloud your mind as you struggle to go forward in your life as a single person. You wonder if you could ever trust anyone enough again to re-marry or whether you can stand alone carrying all the responsibility in your life without running into the arms of another person just because you find yourself so needy?

How long you were married can determine the size of your loss. Who gets the house, furniture, cars, and even the dog? The children have now become the biggest prize of all, and you find yourself fighting to keep the dream of being a mother or father alive even if it means destroying your ex to do so. You realize you have lost your loving disposition only to have morphed into an angry, bitter, jealous, vindictive person you would not even like. You start to tell your side of your story to friends and family members to get their support, and the lines of battle have been drawn where each person is fighting to keep something of what they worked for so their loss will not hurt them for years to come.

Divorce is a messy business, and when a Christian finds themselves in one, they do not always know how to act in an authentic way that would be considered Christian. They know from reading their Bibles that they are supposed to love, forgive, and to show mercy, but all they feel is anger, hurt, resentment, and unforgiveness. All very normal and natural emotions, but no place to live.

There are many stages a person can experience in the death of their marriage. Denial, negotiation, anger, grief, depression, and finally, acceptance.

Denial is shock and disbelief that you are experiencing something you never anticipated. You hoped beyond hope that a miracle would happen to save your marriage. That your spouse would see the error of their ways and realize that they love you too much to think of a living a life without you. Then the day comes where you are standing in front of a judge, and not a preacher, and your spouse is swearing before God and man that they no longer want to be in a marriage with you and are entirely convinced that this is the right thing to do, for them at least.

Negotiation happens as you frantically work to avoid the threat of divorce, especially if you are the person not wanting to be divorced. You try to reason, offer solutions, are willing to compromise more than you should, appeal to friends and family members to talk some sense into your mate, etc.

Anger and rage come when you realize that you have

been rejected by the person who swore to love you all the days of their life. And even though life had gotten hard, weren't they supposed to love you in good times and bad, till death do you part? Trust issues arise, and now you see pure evil in this person you once thought you could never live without, and you cannot understand why you should fight for your marriage any longer. It is a sad day for the person who wanted to keep fighting for their marriage.

When you finally realize that divorce is inevitable, you will enter into the grieving stage. **Grieving** over the death of your marriage will be similar to experiencing grief after a loved one dies. The magnitude of your grief will depend on how much of your heart you invested in your marriage and into your ex. I have seen people never get over this loss. They get stuck in their grief and go on to live sad lives. Although grief is normal and natural, it is no place to linger any longer than needed as grief has the potential to turn into bitterness.

Depression happens because you can't see how you can ever be happy again. You don't know how you will make it alone, and you feel lonely. Your life has changed, and you're sure it is not for good. Your self-image has been damaged robbing you of the needed confidence to go forward. You have entered into a dark night of the soul.

But in time, comes **acceptance.** Even though a person finally accepts their divorce, that does not mean that they stop their feelings for their ex-spouses. Not even in the slightest. They can find themselves caught between still loving them and intense hatred as they watch them go forward in life perhaps with another person. Core feelings of self-worth and even your security will be rocked for years to come as you wonder how to be happy again. You wonder if you should do the same and find another person to make you feel good about yourself, but you don't know if you could trust anyone that much again. And even though you know you are broken and confused, you also know that you hate feeling this way and will do what you have to do to stop the pain.

This is the death of a dream, and you will find yourself grieving over it for some time to come. How to pick up the pieces and start over again is beyond your understanding, and you feel numb as you go through the motions of living life. Tenderness is needed even though you are unable to give it as you only feel harshness in your heart. I believe the grieving process is necessary and although it can be delayed due to responsibilities of work or caring for your children. Even so, you should find a way to pour out your heart to God telling Him the good bad and the ugly about how you are feeling and doing. Only when you know the Father has heard your complaints, and feel His love and acceptance once again, can the healing process truly begin.

Chapter 4
Dealing with Grief and Depression

Grieving

Even as a person would grieve over the death of a loved one, they will experience grief over the loss of a marriage. I don't think anyone can understand the bonding that takes place in a marriage. Separating two people who have been joined together by God can be similar to separating two pieces of paper that had been glued together. If you were ever to try to separate those two pieces of paper from each other, the damage to each article would be quite visible. Each paper would still have parts of the other attached to them never to be the same again.

This is how it can feel after a divorce. How do you go back to who you were before the marriage? You simply can't. Parts of your ex will go with you into your future. How much will be determined by the level of unity and the merging of your collective lives you experienced during the marriage. Children, finances, houses, cars, property, friends, family members. And then there is the heart. Were you all in? Or, did you hold back some of your heart? The level of your commitment will determine the level of your loss.

While in this stage, people will tend to want to pull the bed covers over their head and hide. They are afraid to go out into public for fear their tears will start to flow at the slightest trigger without their ability to stop them. Emotional triggers can happen in a grocery store, taking a walk in the woods, watching a movie that reminds you of what you just went through, attending a wedding or celebrating your parents' wedding anniversary. For me, it would happen when I saw a couple taking a walk, enjoying the evening and holding hands because that was something I really enjoyed doing with my husband when we were married.

Grieving does not have a time limit, and a person cannot predict how long this stage will last. Grieving is something you should not run from, but it is also no place to live. I do not believe it will stop until you decide that it is time to live again. Until that happens, patience will be required of you as well as from those who know you. Friends and family members who have to listen and re-listened to your stories just so you can talk out what happened to you in your marriage. Even so, we all need people to talk to in this life.

Sue's Story

When I went through my divorce, my lawyer told me I was the worst case she had ever seen. I was so very depressed, and the only way I can describe how I was feeling is that I was being ripped apart from the inside out. I felt helpless as I watched my family being destroyed before my eyes. It was by far the most painful thing I have ever been through. I could not get out of bed, read my Bible, or even talk to God. My world as I knew it, was caving in on me.

My sister told me that I was like a soda bottle that had been shaken up and all that poison had to spew out before God could put something back. She said that even though I found myself unable to even read the Bible, I should just say the name Jesus because there is power in His name. There were days I walked around all day just saying "Jesus" over and over again. I also listened to songs that spoke to me. Somedays I would listen to those songs all day long. I was a total wreck.

My lawyer told me about Divorce Care, and I went. I went through two sessions as I needed so much help. I did not even speak for the first three meetings, because I knew that once I opened my mouth, all my pent-up pain would come out and it did. However, once I started talking, I liked it because I was able to share my story with people who could understand what I was going through.

I asked my group leader when the pain would get better. He gave me some good advice. He said that it took a while to get here and it will take some time to get my life back. However, he said that all of my experiences up to this point have been with my ex and that each experience in my future will be without him. He said that after some time, the new experiences of walking down different paths will come stronger to the forefront, and the old ones will start to fade as the new ones emerge. He told me that usually after six months, I would start to feel better. After one year even better, and by two years, I would feel like myself again. What he said was true. My pain began to fade away with time and new experiences and yours will too.

Depression

A simple definition of depression is a loss of hope by varying degrees. A depressed person struggles to believe that things will get better, especially if things have been hard for a long time. Although experiencing depression after a divorce is normal, it is no place to live for very long. If you find that you are stuck in depression, it might be a good idea to seek out professional help.

Time Heals All

As Sue discovered, the pain of divorce lessens with time and new experiences. Time is a great healer when it comes to emotional trauma.

Put Your Hope in God

Another antidote I know of in overcoming depression is hope. *"For I know the thoughts that I think toward you, says the LORD, thoughts of peace and not of evil, to give you a future and a hope."* (Jeremiah 29:11, NKJV) Hope is powerful. The following story describes what I mean by this statement.

Warning: If you're an animal lover (which I am), you're going to hate the following story, but try to glean God's truth from it anyway. To encourage me in a trial I was going through, a friend called to tell me about a scientific research study she had heard about. To discover what caused living creatures to persevere, scientists placed two dogs in two different glass containers filled with water to see which dog would survive the longest. One of the dogs had lived in the wild for his entire life, and the other dog had been raised and cared for by his owner. She asked me which dog I thought had survived the longest. Guessing, I replied, "The domesticated dog, because he was submissive." She said, "You're right, but here's the reason why. The domesticated dog persevered longer because he kept expecting his master to rescue him from this trial as he always had." *"I waited patiently for the LORD; he inclined to me and heard my cry. He drew me up from the pit of destruction, out of the miry bog, and set my feet upon a rock, making my steps secure."* (Psalm 40:1–2, ESV)

Just as the domesticated dog persevered because he trusted [hoped] in his master to save him, we are to continue in faith, trusting that our Faithful Master will come and deliver us. Hope causes a person to persevere [believe] when there isn't any visible reason to continue to believe. *"I would have despaired unless I had believed that I would see the goodness of the LORD in the land of the living."* (Psalm 27:13, NASB). When you are in a trial, and you have done all that you know to do, then you must continue to stand [waiting with expectation] for the Lord's deliverance. This will require an attitude of persistence.

Guard Your Words and Thoughts

*"Do not conform to the pattern of this world, **but be transformed by the renewing of your mind**. Then you will be able to test and approve what God's will is—his good, pleasing and perfect will."* (Romans 12:2, emphasis added).

When my daughter was a toddler, she would watch

"Sesame Street" on TV. This program described a person's emotions to the children, and I caught her practicing those emotions when we were in the car. Looking in my rear-view mirror, I would watch her saying, "I am happy," and then I saw a smile on her face. Then she would say next, "I am sad." And she would change her countenance to be sad. She repeated these phrases over and over again until we reached our destination. After a few times, I noticed that whichever phrase she ended on was how she acted once I turned the car off. This is funny but true for all of us.

"For as he thinks within himself, so he is." (Proverbs 23:7 NASB). Watch what you put into your mind through watching TV or through the friends you hang out with because they will influence your thoughts, and those thoughts will eventually become your actions. Don't believe me? Notice what happens to a person who watches too much news these days. I find they become angry, frustrated, and negative people.

I refuse to watch or listen to doom and gloom because I know it will get into my inner man and depress me. Instead, I love to watch true stories of people who overcame great odds to do the impossible. After I watch their stories, I realize that most accomplishments come through adversity. They are rarely just handed to you. How bad do you want it? Can you endure a season of suffering to get it? The answer to that question will determine your outcome.

After my divorce, I knew I had to get rid of my negativity if I wanted to be successful in the new business I had started. So, I began to watch one inspirational speaker a day on YouTube. It has greatly helped me. This is another principle that you must do to experience the truth in it. I don't think I will ever stop doing this because the benefits have been incredible.

Get a New Perspective

I have experienced bouts of depression throughout my life, wondering if things would ever get easier or more enjoyable. Whenever I would complain to God about how I was feeling, He would bring to my attention another person who had it worse than me. Afterward, I asked God to forgive me, and I prayed for the person he pointed out to me.

While raising my children, I took them with me on mission trips to Mexico City where we would minister to children living in the garbage dumps. Due to this experience, I have heard my daughter often say, "My worse day would be considered someone else's best day." Sometimes we just need a new perspective to help us fight our depression.

The Power of Gratitude and Giving

Take a real look at your life and give God thanks for what you do have because trust me there are those out there who would love to have what you have. Then go out and be kind to another human being who needs your kindness. You will be amazed at how good this will make you feel. *"It is more blessed to give than to receive."* (Acts 20:35)

I'll never forget the day I walked into a United States Post Office upset and stressed out, trying to control two very active toddlers. When I walked up to the teller, she looked at me and said, "You look like you are having a bad day. How can I help you?" Her words of kindness melted my heart, and the stress I was experiencing lifted. I was so grateful for her kind words. We can all offer kind words to each other. It is an easy thing to do that may impact a person far more than you can realize.

Go for a walk

Physical exercise is vital in fighting depression. Why? Because it has been proven that physical activity produces chemicals in the body called endorphins. These endorphins give a person a positive feeling. I especially love to take a walk in the woods or by a lake mostly because I feel God's presence and His peace in nature. Exercise also works to improve a person's self-esteem making it doubly useful.

Chapter 5
Denise's Story

I can honestly say that 2005 was the worse year of my life. That's a lot to say because I had already experienced incest and cancer before 2005. However, what came next, I could never have predicted because my ex-husband was a master manipulator and liar.

It all started in January when I got a phone call from the police department asking me to accept phone charges from my husband. He was in jail because they had caught him soliciting a 15-year-old for sex. At first, I did not believe it because I thought my husband to be a man of God, but once the evidence was presented, I had to accept the truth and deal with it. I was numb with unbelief, embarrassed, ashamed, sad, and angry, too. I think I experienced every dark emotion there was to experience. My self-image as a woman was damaged as I questioned why my husband felt I was not enough and had to look outside our marriage for sex. I wondered who had I been married to for ten years? I no longer felt I knew him.

I confronted him, but he always knew how to manipulate me, and soon enough, I forgave him. I had four children depending on us, and I needed to believe we could overcome this. We started counseling with our pastor, and I thought he was doing better only to have another bomb dropped on me.

We had just gotten home from Wednesday night Bible study when there was a knock on the door. I answered the door, and two detectives asked for my husband. Without saying much, they took my husband to the police station, where they charged him with molesting two boys from our church. I could not breathe. I wanted to die right there. I had no idea any of this was happening because I had been fighting cancer and was sick with treatment on top of taking care of our four children and I never knew what had been happening in my home.

Depression and suicidal thoughts tortured my mind day and night, but I had four children depending on me and could not quit on them. My kids kept me going. They became my lifeline. I fell to my knees, crying out to God even though I could not see any way possible to escape from my hell.

Reality came fast as overnight I was without money and homeless because I had only been working a part-time job and was unable to pay the rent. I knew I had to figure out how to support my children fast as I had no family to help me out. I did have some church friends who offered to help me, but I was so ashamed and embarrassed I hesitated to go to church wondering if they thought I had known what my husband had been doing. I was sure they were angry with me because I had failed to stop him, but I had been too sick and too tired to notice any signs of his predatory behavior.

With all that was happening, I didn't really know how the Lord could help me, but if He didn't help me, we would soon be living in the streets cold, hungry and afraid and here's how the Lord led me "step by step" through my nightmare.

After praying for me, a woman from my church felt the Lord wanted me to apply for a government job. The only government job I could think of was the local military base, so I went there to ask if they were hiring. It turned out that they were, and I was hired on the spot. The job I was hired for was a three-month temp job that never ended. I was paid a good wage, but it was not enough to support us because they took out money every paycheck to pay for my health insurance.

When the people I worked with heard my story, they showed me compassion and did what they could to encourage me. I told my friend that I was being shown favor at work and she suggested that I ask my boss if I could sell some snacks from my desk. I asked, and he said yes! My friend took me to Aldi's, and she bought me a variety of snacks to sell. I placed them on my desk, and they sold out in two days. I was so grateful to my fellow employees because they chose to buy snacks from me instead of the vending machines. I re-invested the money I earned to buy more snacks to sell and used the rest to help cover my living expenses. It was through selling those snacks that I was finally able to squeak by.

A year or so later, this same woman said she could see I had an entrepreneur spirit on me and asked me to think of a business to start. I was racking my mind to figure out what I could do when she noticed a bracelet I was wearing. She asked me about it, and when I told her I had made it, she asked me what I needed to make more. My hobby turned into an addiction that made money and kept my mind from the dark places I could have so quickly gone into.

It's been fourteen years since this all started, and I am re-married, have eight grandchildren, a growing business, and all my children are successfully pursuing their lives. I can honestly say that I am blessed beyond blessed by all the Lord has done for me and what the devil meant for harm, God used for my good to give me a testimony of His ability to deliver this humble woman from what could have easily been a defeated and sad life.

Chapter 6
Dealing with Anger

There is a saying that goes, "Hurting people, hurt people." I have found this to be true in my life. The hurts I experienced in my life turned me into an angry person. I would lash out, returning evil for evil. I knew it was wrong and did not want to act like this but ended up doing so anyway because my harsh circumstances had changed me. I reasoned that we would expect a dog to growl at us if we had continually been mistreating it and that's true. However, God calls us to a higher standard and gives us His grace to live a godly life despite our circumstances. The following story is what the Lord did to help me heal.

Soon after my divorce, I was anguishing over all the wrongs I perceived my ex had done to me, and I was angry. The more I thought about what had happened, the angrier I became. I didn't like feeling angry, but I could not figure out what to do to get rid of it. Because even after the divorce, our encounters with each other only reminded me of what had happened, and I ended up angry all over again. I felt I had experienced a considerable injustice and that my life had been disrespected by the man who was to respect, love, and cherish me.

This went on for some time until I had an encounter with the Holy Spirit during one of my morning devotions. I was lamenting over my failed marriage and telling the Lord all that I was feeling. I think I might have said, "How can I get rid of my anger when I am still suffering? I think I have a right to be angry." The Holy Spirit didn't argue with me. In fact, He agreed with me. He said to my heart, "Yes, you do have a right to be angry. Many wrongs happened to you, but I am asking you to give up your right to be angry for me." What could I say? I guess the Lord knew how to let me know He had heard me and still cause me to want to change, if not for me, for Him. That encounter helped me to see my situation from a higher vantage point. I saw it from the Lord's eyes. My eyes were opened, and in light of all he suffered for me when I was the one who caused His suffering, I knew I really had no right to be angry at all.

Did my anger entirely end that day? Sadly, it did not. But each time it rose up, I went back to His words and quieted my soul and soon enough I was doing much better.

Responding Versus Reacting

In the past, when I felt disrespected, I did not respond like I should have because I was a damaged person. It took me years to learn how to respond instead of reacting to bad behaviors, and I am sad to say that I did not discover this while I was married. Unlike me, a healthy person with a healthy self-image will not allow another person to treat them disrespectfully repeatedly. They will stand their ground and communicate that what was just said or done cannot continue and if the other person refuses to respect them, then they must withdraw until the matter has been resolved safely. This may mean ending a relationship, and an insecure person who has self-esteem issues will have difficulty doing this.

Love and Forgiveness

"Love your neighbor as yourself." If you bite and devour each other, watch out or you will be destroyed by each other." (Galatians 5:14-15). In every divorce, two people will have to choose between destroying each other or finding a way to have peace between them. For me, peace is everything. Peace didn't come overnight between Tony and me, but it did come, and I give God all the credit for helping us to achieve it.

"Bear with each other and forgive one another if any of you has a grievance against someone. Forgive as the Lord forgave you" (Colossians 3:13). God asks us to forgive each other even as He freely forgave us. This will almost always be a process, especially if the hurts go deep. Jesus is our example. He forgave those who crucified Him even though there was no wrongdoing on his part. And there it is. Because all of us have sinned and are guilty of at least some wrongdoing, His example leaves us without an excuse for refusing to forgive others when they have sinned against us.

Whenever I need to forgive someone, I start by praying for them. Through prayer, God enables me to see that person through His eyes, and this new vision helps to soften my heart.

Forgiveness Does not Always Mean Restoration.

We are not asked to be restored to a person who has not repented but we do have to forgive them whether they repent or not and place them into the hands of the Lord, allowing Him alone to be their judge.

Unforgiveness leads to bitterness, and bitterness leads to sickness. Although I had other reasons to forgive, this was the most compelling reason that caused me to forgive Tony. The human body does not function well when upset all the time. Think about it. Do you like feeling angry all the time? I know I don't. I wanted to be free to love and to laugh. Because Tony and I both chose to forgive, we can laugh and be at ease during our family get-togethers.

In every family or relationship, there will always be the need to forgive. The easier it is for you to forgive and forget, will determine the quality of your relationships. I will say that Tony made it easier for me to forgive him with his acts of kindness towards me.

Since our divorce, Tony and I have learned how to say what we have to say to each other when dealing with an issue between us, and then let it go. We understand that the bond of peace among us must be protected and that sometimes means overlooking an offense. *"Above all, love each other deeply, because love covers over a multitude of sins."* (1 Peter 4:8)

Determine that, as far as possible, you will live in peace with the people around you. Even so, there will be times that you must withdraw from a person who wants to involve you in their drama all the time, who stays angry and upsets everyone around them. *"They must turn from evil and do good; they must seek peace and pursue it."* (1 Peter 3:11)

Letting Go

Alongside the process of forgiving comes letting go. You simply cannot reclaim your life until you let go. You must release your ex from all blame and all future expectations. Then go forward to find your life. This will most likely be a process. To help you in this process, avoid stalking your ex on Facebook. Closing the door on that relationship will help you look forward and not backward. Then trust the Lord to lead and guide both you and your ex into His will for your futures. **Life is not over, just different.**

Anger That Motivates

"An **angry** *person stirs up conflict, and a hot-tempered person commits many sins"* (Proverbs 29:22) *"In your anger do not sin"* (Ephesians 4:26)

The Bible clearly teaches us that unchecked anger leads to sin. We are warned to stay away from anger when it does not produce righteousness (and it rarely does). Instead, God would have us exercise self-control over our emotions. But there is an anger that motivates a person to act to bring forth justice. An example of righteous anger is displayed when Jesus went through the temple, turning over tables and driving the people out with a whip because they had turned His Father's house into a den of thieves. God will give a person righteous anger that will motivate a person to right wrongs. The following story is an example of a person's anger motivating them to act to correct a wrong situation.

Joyce's Story

For years I experienced verbal, emotional, and sometimes physical abuse in my "Christian" marriage. I said this because all this abuse happened while we went to church every Sunday. I had married an angry man who would bully me into submission. Confronting him made him angry, so I avoided it. It didn't matter how kindly I tried to present the truth to him, he would only become angry then turn to attack me to get the conversation off of him. He would taunt me saying, "So you think you are a Christian? You are as angry as me. So, how good of a Christian are you?" I would get angry and would start yelling at him just to be heard. Even though I loved him, I also profoundly disrespected him for his treatment of me.

We had four children, and he was our primary income. My lack of income left me with no real options to get out of my abusive marriage. That was until my children were old enough to allow me to work again. My income gave me some confidence to take more actions. I didn't plan what happened next, though. I can't remember what the fight was about, but I do remember getting really angry and making an instant decision to kick him out of the house. I picked up some of his clothes went to the back porch and threw them into the yard, screaming "Get out!"

I went back into the house, and the TV preacher I had been listening to was yelling, "Kick the bum out!" No lie. That's just what he said. I think the Lord knew I needed to hear this to keep me strong in my decision as I was already feeling guilty for being so angry. Afterward, I made an appointment with my pastor to tell him what had happened. I informed him my intentions were not to get divorced but to save my marriage. He agreed and gave me his permission to separate from my husband.

My husband would come over to the house, and I would refuse to be with him and suggested that he could spend some time with the kids. This ended up being so good for the kids because they had always wanted his attention and now, he wanted to be with them. It took six months, but he eventually wanted to come back home. We still had more to go through, but it was a chance to make our marriage work again the way God intended for it to be.

Chapter 7
Children and Divorce

"My people will live in peaceful dwelling places, in secure homes, in undisturbed places of rest." (Isaiah 32:18) Our homes should be havens of peace. It is a blessing from God. That being said, fighting in our homes stresses out our children as well as the parents. For that reason, divorce for the sake of peace can be better than staying in a marriage filled with hate and anger. However, quite often a divorce does not end the fighting. It sometimes increases it.

Couples who continue to fight after their divorce can use their kids as pawns to manipulate or get back at their ex. They can use tactics like bad mouthing their ex in front of their children by telling them all the bad things their other parent did so they will take sides with them, use their children to inform on their ex., ask them to deliver messages to your ex like, "Tell your father …" or "Tell your mother…" All of these behaviors put your child in a situation they don't want to be in. They don't want to take sides; they want to be loved by both their parents. They can't fix anything and yet feel pressured to be part of a situation that is out of their control. So, stop venting in front of your children. It's not fair. *"A fool gives full vent to his spirit, but a wise man quietly holds it back."* (Proverbs 29:11 ESV)

At the same time, all you can do is to control your own emotions and appeal to your ex to do the same for the sake of the kids. If your ex continues to spew out anger, do your best not to engage. If they are vindictive, you may have to have a third-party advocate for you, but the goal is to find a way to have peace between you for the sake of the kids. Even so, you are only responsible for your actions. *"Make every effort to live in peace with everyone."* Hebrews 12:14

"But I tell you, love your enemies and pray for those who persecute you." (Matthew 5:44) If you need to communicate with an angry ex, it might be best to do it through email. At least you will get to say what you need to say without having a fight. But before you send that email, re-read it to make sure you are not making things worse. I rewrote so many emails, and I was glad that I had email available to me so that I could be more careful with my words. A good rule to follow is never to send an email when you are angry and walk away from it for a day before you hit the send button.

What a Child Needs After a Divorce

After your divorce, your children will need to feel safe and secure, engage in normal activities, and believe you love and accept them no matter what. They need to be just kids free from adult burdens. To meet your child's needs, you may have to lay your life down, especially right after the divorce. Let them know you will always be there for them. They may also need to understand that the divorce was not their fault as many kids feel it is.

For example, after my sister's divorce, she put her seven-year-old son on her lap, held his hands, looked into his eyes, and said to him, "I want you to know that I will be the one taking care of you from now on, and I am never ever, ever, going to leave you. I will make sure that you have everything you need. You will always have food to eat, clothes to wear and a place to live. I promise you that you will not have to worry about anything because I am always going to take care of you."

I am sad when I see couples get divorced and then go on to live their lives without making their children know that they are their top priority. I have also seen divorces where the parents continue to be there for their children after the divorce, and these children are secure and go on to live healthy adult lives. It can be accomplished but not without being intentional about it.

On the flip side, don't overindulge your children after a divorce just because you feel guilty. Kids are smart and may start to manipulate you once you open that door. Just be there for them and keep things as normal as possible. The goal should be to have two loving parents raising their children after a divorce. If that is not possible, then offer them one loving, stable parent.

Abandonment Issues

In every divorce, children and adults will experience feelings of being abandoned by the people they needed the most. This can shake their world for years to come. A divorce where the children never knew there was a problem until the day they were told their parents were divorcing can be especially confusing to them. They never saw their parents fight during their marriage and wonder why their parents are divorcing. I can only imagine these children will question their future relationships, wondering if the person they are married to won't also abandon them without notice. These divorced parents will have to give their children some kind of explanation according to their child's ability to understand combined with ample communications of their commitment to being there for them. I believe these feelings of abandonment can be overcome if their parents continue to show their children that their well-being is their top priority.

Chapter 8
Additional Places to Heal

Before you can successfully go forward, you may need to be healed from the trauma you experienced during your marriage and divorce. Although I have already addressed several issues where a divorced person will need healing, in this chapter, I am listing more core issues that can scar a person's life.

You are Valuable

This issue is the hardest one for me to talk about because it exposes the deepest part of me: my need to feel loved and cherished. When the man I loved and served for 34 years divorced me, it screamed how little he valued me, the very person he was to value the most. By divorcing me, he was saying he would be better off living life without me, and that hurt. This rejection created in me intense anger I could not hide.

And there it is. We all want to be loved and cherished by the people closest to us. When we don't get the love we think we deserve, we can find ourselves looking for it in other places. Some turn to careers, others go on shopping sprees buying things they can't afford, and many try to find love through various relationships. These other sources will put a bandage on your wounds for a time, but if your value is not rooted in God, all other ways will merely cover up your insecurities, only to have them resurface at a later date.

Hurting, I told myself that one man's garbage could

become another man's treasure, and I found myself desperately wanting to prove to my ex-husband the truth of that statement. Had I done that, I would not be enjoying the life I have. Instead, I had to quiet my soul and choose to believe that God valued me.

To help establish myself in His love, I studied the Song of Songs, a song about King Solomon's love for a Shulamite girl. Most Bible scholars agree that this letter is about marital love, but it also communicates the love God has for His people. As I read these Scriptures, it was as if the Lord was speaking to the deepest part of me and not just to the Shulamite woman. God said I was lovely, even though I knew I was dark (from sin, Song 1:5). The Holy Spirit wooed me with His words, *"You have ravished my heart, My sister, my spouse; You have ravished my heart With one look of your eyes."* (4:9) My soul responded, *"My beloved is mine and I am his."* (2:16)

These Scriptures humanized God in a way I never imagined. When God declared Himself to be *ravished* by me, I came to understand that I could hurt His heart by preferring another before Him. I treasure those intimate moments with Him and find myself wanting to cleave to Him. My life is bound up in His, and I am no longer my own. Because of His love for me, I joyfully submit to His will for my life. I trust Him above all others.

The Need for Validation

If you feel you have been wronged in your marriage, you will want others to agree with you. To get their agreement, you will present your case to them by exposing your ex-spouse's sins against you. You may even ask your children to side with you. Although this is very understandable, it will cause more harm than good. Children should never have to choose sides against either of their parents. They naturally want to be loved by both their mother and their father and are already traumatized enough by your divorce.

The Bible tells us that Jesus refused to defend Himself when he was wrongfully accused. Instead, He trusted His Father to vindicate Him. God challenged me to trust Him to do the same for me. What a challenge this was. I must confess, I did not come close to being very successful, but I still had to keep trying.

We all need to talk out our issues to get another person's point of view or support. I was no exception. In time, I found people I could safely talk to. These people patiently listened to me without judging me or forcing me to do things their way. They knew I had to work some things out and gave me the space to do so. They also challenged me to do better when they saw I could. When talking to others about your ex-spouse, you will know in your heart whether you are talking to work out an issue or to destroy the person who hurt you.

Victim or Victor?

If you continue for too long to defend yourself by telling everyone how your ex-spouse wronged you, you may find some solace in the people who empathize with you, but you will also stay in a position of weakness. You cannot be a victim and a victor at the same time. You must choose which one you want to be and then live like the one you choose.

None of us can make another person do anything they do not want to do. Not willingly, that is. All we can do is make godly choices for ourselves and pray for God to change their hearts. Then we must leave the results to God. I did not do this. I wish I had, but I was so damaged and didn't realize how broken I really was.

Separating for the Sake of Peace

My biggest regret is that I let my anger get hold of me, and more often than not, I returned evil for evil. I cannot say that I acted like a Christian in all of this, and it is to my real shame. I did this in front of my children, the ones I was to be an example to. I guess I reasoned that they could see what I was going through and would not think less of me for misbehaving, but that was a wrong thought.

After the divorce, I tried to figure out how I could have done things differently. The truth is, I could have decided to separate from my husband for the sake of peace and perhaps to save my marriage (1 Corinthians 7). But because I was so fearful of not being able to make it without his help, I stayed in a marriage that became toxic to both of us.

Separating will only save the marriage if, after spending time away from each other, two people decide they really do want to be married and are willing to make the needed changes. If your spouse doesn't decide in favor of marriage, then the marriage is most likely over, apart from an act of God.

In our salvation covenant with Jesus, we are never forced to stay in a relationship with Him. We were free to enter into it, and we are free to leave. That is what free choice is all about. In the same way, when your spouse decides to leave the marriage, you are to allow them to go.

Denise's Story

One year after a terrible divorce, I met a married a man who made me feel loved and valued. He stood over six feet tall, and his size made me feel safe and secure. I knew I could trust this kind man and looked forward to his influence on my children. But what happened next took me by surprise. My older children did not accept him and started to work against him. As a single mom, I had been my children's only advocate, and the mama bear in me didn't know how to protect them and support my husband too. It was clear that he felt disrespected by them, and they felt controlled by a man who was not their father.

The fighting got so bad that we were considering divorce. I talked to my Christian friend about my situation when she suggested that instead of divorcing, I should separate from him for the sake of peace and return to the marriage when it was possible. I took her advice and moved out with my children. Not an easy path to follow or to explain to anyone else, but I knew my heart, I wanted my marriage. I also knew my husband could not handle the disrespect he was getting from my children and was resenting me for not siding with him.

Three years later, my older three children had reached the age where they could move out, and they did. My son joined the military, and my two daughters married. My youngest son did not experience the same rebellion my older children had as he had been a baby when his father and I had divorced. I am happy to say the advice of my friend saved my marriage, and we are once again united and enjoying our marriage without all the pressures a blended family can bring to a marriage.

Dealing with Shame

Because I had always believed that God would heal my marriage, I had never considered ever being divorced. So, when I became divorced, I went from being a married Christian woman to being a divorced Christian woman overnight.

To be honest, I didn't know how my new status as a Christian divorcee could ever bring God glory. I was embarrassed about being divorced and no longer felt qualified to tell people that God's ways were the best way to live. My example surely didn't prove it. I was confused as to how I could ever bring God glory without being successfully married.

The shame a person feels will cause them to hide even though it is impossible to keep a divorce private for any length of time. The shame of it will make a person feel like they have a scarlet letter tattooed on their forehead for all to see and judge. A very humbling and humiliating experience.

Stay Faithful after Disappointments

Even though I was disappointed that God had not healed my marriage, I could not quit following Him because of all my past experiences with Him. Those experiences had entirely convinced me that His ways were right even though I had failed to achieve His best. Following this reasoning, I chose to keep doing what I knew was right and leave the results to Him. That is all any of us can do when our circumstances are not what we hoped they would be.

Interestingly enough, when a Christian experiences a failure or life-changing trauma, this is where other people will watch to see if they will stick to their profession of faith in Jesus. I know I waited to see what others would do when it got tough to adhere to their standards. I wanted to see if that person really believed what they said because it is easy to say some things and hard to stick to our words when life gets tough. I think it is a better measure of what a person truly believes than what they do when everything is going great.

Dealing with Guilt

You may not have been the person who did the most damage in your marriage, but all of us know where we missed it. Guilty feelings for the part we did play in the demise of our marriages can only be healed through confession. James, chapter 5, advises us to confess our sins so we may be healed. Asking for forgiveness for what we did wrong is all a person can do. It can be hard to do this when your ex-has did not ask you to forgive them for their offenses, and this is where humility comes into play. If you cannot confess to your ex, find a safe person, and receive healing through confession.

After you have confessed your part in your divorce, you must ask God to forgive you and choose to forgive yourself as well. If you don't do these two things, you will continue to experience guilt and shame. We live in a fallen world and are subject to failures. Our failures serve to keep us humble and dependent upon God's mercy and grace.

Loss of Purpose

A good portion of today's church is made up of divorced people, and they wonder if they have forfeited their chance to serve the Lord in the Church, using their God-given gifts and talents.

So, can God use a divorced person to accomplish His will? In John 4, Jesus chose a divorced Samaritan woman to evangelize her whole town. He reached out to her knowing she had been divorced five times and was currently living with a man. Why did Jesus choose her? Could it be that she would be a fantastic example of God's power to transform a person's life?

Even today, we have many examples of men and women who were delivered from a life of sin to become inspirational preachers. 2 Corinthians 1:4 says it is [God], *"who comforts us in all our troubles, so that we can comfort those in any trouble with the comfort we ourselves receive from God."* And there it is. When our family and friends see us struggle with the same issues they sometimes struggle with, they will watch to see if we will stay faithful, because they want to know if we really believe what we profess.

A person's divorce cannot remove God's call on their life. Romans 11:29 says that *"God's gifts and his call are irrevocable."* When I wondered if God's call on my life had been forfeited because of my divorce, the Lord was quick to tell me that He had not divorced me and to keep trusting Him to fulfill all the promises He had given me.

How to Deal with Loss

The loss experienced in a divorce can be tremendous, depending on how much you invested in the marriage. There will be the loss of finances, shared property, custody of children, dreams, etc. For women who stayed at home to raise the children, the divorce can put them into poverty, only to watch their ex-spouse succeed in the careers they sacrificially helped them achieve.

I remember praying, crying out for the Lord to take all my loss and to somehow use it for His glory. I needed to believe that the pain I was experiencing would not be in vain. The Lord promised to give me beauty in exchange for my ashes, and He has. Joy does come in the morning even though you may have to go through the dark night of the soul to get it.

Fearing Future Failures

The only way I was able to overcome my fear of future

failure and the possibility of experiencing more shame and disappointment, was when I truly believed that the Lord was still for me, so who could be against me? (Romans 8:31) I did not have enough self-confidence to move forward on my own without the Lord communicating to me that He had my back. I was painfully aware of my limitations and all of my weaknesses. But even so, the Lord asked me to go forward once again and to trust Him to make a way whenever I could not see a way. I went ahead by faith, and He has kept to His promise to make a way. His faithfulness has never failed me, and I will continue to go forward, trusting in His promise to me.

Anxiety Attacks

With all the unknown and uncertainty of my new life, I would experience stress and panic attacks. I had learned years ago to say scriptures that applied to my situation out loud and to repeat them like I meant them until my fear lessened. The Bible says that faith comes by hearing and hearing by the word of God. (Romans 10:17) When we speak scriptures out loud, we will hear those scriptures, and there is power in the spoken word of God. I cannot remember how I came upon this truth, but once I discovered it, I practiced it. It works! At the same time, if you continue to speak words of fear and doubt, you will hear those words and fear will enter into you.

Whenever I see a person suffering from fear, I speak a scripture verse that I know to be true and I speak it out loud in their presence as boldly and with as much confidence as I can muster up. My verbal confidence in God's word will produce faith in the person suffering from fear. I never worry with them. Instead, I encourage them to believe that God is able and will make a way for them even when it looks like there is no way.

What is the worst that can happen? It almost never does. So, why do we find ourselves going there before we give God a chance to show us what He can do. Slow down, quiet your emotions, and let God be God.

Chapter 9
Flying Solo

It wasn't too long after my divorce that I came face to face with the following question. Who am I? I had been a wife for 34 years and a mother for over 25 years, and when my divorce happened, both of these roles seemingly disappeared overnight, and I was thrown into a personal identity crisis. Who was I without my ex? Our lives had been so intertwined for so long that I could not remember who I was before him. Did any of that girl still exist? I had not wanted to be divorced and had fought for my marriage longer than I should have. Now I was faced with trying to figure out what to do next? I possessed so many questions with no real answers.

The Beginning of Answers to Come

Five days after my divorce I decided to take a trip I had always wanted to take, and I packed up my motorcycle and traveled 400 miles away to see my sister who lived in Black Mountain, North Carolina. It was my divorce trip. As I rode down the expressway with the wind blowing on my face and my troubles behind me, I felt the freedom a motorcycle ride can give you. It was during this ride and trip that I had some alone time to think about what had just happened. The trip brought me to a safe and happy place. I played in the rivers, took long walks through the woods, and heard from the Lord. His voice quieted my soul, and I returned, knowing that He would go back with me. I was not alone, and that gave me the confidence I needed to go on.

It wasn't too long after my divorce that the Holy Spirit warned me to be careful not to react in ways that could potentially hurt me. This is where divorcees can go wild, trying to experience life to its fullness again. I was tempted to do just that but felt a huge check in my spirit stopping me. Knowing that I had to find some kind of life to replace the one that had been taken from me, I asked the Lord to give me something to do that would satisfy some of my neediness and He did. He led me step by step continuing to encourage me to stay solo, not date, and to trust Him instead to meet my emotional needs that only relationships can meet. Looking back, I can see the wisdom in His instructions.

I Just Can't Get Any Satisfaction

It should come as no surprise that insurance companies have classified newly divorced people to be high risks. When a person has a traumatic change in their lives, it will make them very unstable. They will start to question all the rules they used to live by. Rules that were supposed to keep their lives from going down the toilet. Then, when their divorce happens, rebelliousness enters in, and they will throw out those rules and rush into anything that makes them feel alive, wanted, valued, and desirable. They will search for a way to get their life back on track to how they hoped it would be.

It's hard to stand still and do nothing when you feel your life is passing you by. However, that may be what is needed for a time. When I was first divorced, I immediately knew that if I were to make it, I would need to find a life that would replace some of the loss I just experienced and bring me some amount of personal satisfaction which would keep me out of trouble. The trouble I knew I was capable of if I did not find healthy ways to meet my neediness.

A newly divorced person's flesh will be screaming for satisfaction from years of neglect or abuse. Going wild is a very natural but potentially dangerous response as one day you may wake up to find yourself in a worse place and out of God's will. Guilt and shame will come upon you, and you will want to hide from God and other believers. But I know God's love for you will cause Him to chase you down. He won't judge or condemn you, but He will ask you to change directions. And when you do, you will be stronger and wiser because you just learned what not to do and now you can share your wisdom with another person going through a divorce.

Loneliness

People can die from loneliness. It is proven to be more dangerous than smoking cigarettes to a person's health. In the book of Genesis 2:18, God declared, *"it is not good for the man to be alone."* Then He went on to take a rib from Adam's side to create Eve. Afterward, God said, *"That is why a man leaves his father and mother and is united to his wife, and they become one flesh."* (Genesis 2:24) We were created for intimate fellowship with God and man. Given these undeniable facts, this one issue must be addressed after a divorce healthily, or it will get addressed maybe in a not so healthy way.

I remember the tagline that went with the sitcom Cheers,

"where everybody knows your name." We all need to connect with other people, and Facebook isn't going to do the job. Face to face encounters with other humans is best. We all want to be seen, listened to, and valued by our loved ones. Relationships and community are what make people the happiest.

Divorce Care Groups

Attending a Divorce Care Group will give you a chance to talk to other people who have been recently divorced. These groups are usually facilitated by people who are divorced and have the heart to help others walk through the healing process. My sister, who was extremely depressed and confused after her divorce, went through the program and said it was the one thing that helped her the most through her healing process. She advises, "You have to find a place to spew the poison out of you after your divorce, and you should not do this with family members, and the sooner you go to one of these groups, the better you will be." She believed in it so much that she became a facilitator of her own group for several years. To find a group in your area, do a google search. I found several groups located within 10 miles of where I live.

Friends

"Do not be misled: "Bad company corrupts good character." (1 Cor. 15:33) Be careful of who you hang out with immediately after your divorce. You are more vulnerable than you realize, and if you hang out with the wrong friends, you could end up in the wrong place. I would

92

also strongly suggest that your friends be of the same sex. Although you think its innocent and no big deal to make friends with someone of the opposite sex, many times it will bring out your need to feel desirable and that may take you to a place you don't want to be in. I have witnessed good-hearted Christians try to minister to someone of the opposite sex going through a divorce and in a short amount of time they make an emotional connection with them and start a romantic relationship that was never intended. Wait until you know you are stable and healed enough to make good choices for your future. While you are recovering, same-sex friends will meet your need for fellowship and give you some time to figure out what you want. **You are in the middle of a do-over, so don't make permanent decisions until you know where you want to go.**

Fellowship with God

Soon after my divorce, I heard the Lord assure me that He had not divorced me. When He said this to me, I knew I was not alone. His words made me feel secure in His love, and that knowledge gave me the confidence to go forward even though I did not know where I was going.

One of the ways I asked Him for help was when I felt lonely. During the week, I was busy with work and chores, but when the weekend came, I would have more time on my hands, and that is when I felt especially lonely. I didn't want to appear needy, so I would refrain from inviting myself over to my married friend's or children's houses. I would go on walks by myself to get out of the house, but at the end of the weekend, I felt sad.

"God sets the lonely in families." (Psalms 68:6). I turned to prayer and asked my heavenly Father to provide for my emotional need, and He did. People would ask me to attend their events. I also discovered a place to volunteer and was able to meet new people. And even though I thought about dating just to add some fun to my life, I felt a check in my spirit and never felt God wanted me to date. So, I continued down this road trusting and asking the Lord to meet my continuous need for fellowship.

Join an Interest Group

Today, many social groups have been formed according to a person's interests. They are easy to join and were created to help people meet new people.

Sexual intimacy

You have been used to having intimacy, and now it's gone from your life overnight. It's another hard circumstance that comes with divorce. As Christians, we are not to live, *"in passionate lust like the pagans, who do not know God."* (1 Thessalonians 4:5)

Talking about how to avoid sexual immorality, the apostle Paul says, *"No temptation has overtaken you except what is common to mankind. And God is faithful; he will not let you be tempted beyond what you can bear. But when you are tempted, he will also provide a way out so that you can endure it."*

(1Corithians 10:13) This is another area where it can be hard to be a Christian. I get it. We're all human. Best not to focus on it because what you think about over and over again, you will do.

Reasons for Staying Single After a Divorce

1) To concentrate on your children

If you have younger children, you need to realize that they are also going through a divorce. Their world was turned upside down, and they may be fearful and afraid of what the future holds for them. If you are the parent who has custody, then you will need to lay down your life for a time to make sure you can be there for your kids. You may have to put off grieving or any other personal needs so you can meet their need for security. Bringing strange people into their lives at this time could confuse and frighten them even more than they already are.

2) To discover some of your personal issues.

For the reflection process to have its full effect, it will be important to stand alone. Adding another person into your life at this stage will cause you to consider their wishes, and you could go right back into your old patterns of behavior that you operated in during your last relationship without knowing if those behaviors contributed to your divorce or not.

Most of us can only see what our ex-did to cause our divorce and only after another failed relationship will we realize that maybe we need to change some things too. Standing alone gives you a chance to make your own choices and to see if those choices have consequences attached to them or not. It could be that you will make good choices and enjoy that outcome. If so, this will give you self-confidence in your ability to make good decisions.

3) To give God a chance to restore your marriage.

There are too many stories of God restoring marriages after divorce to not give Him a chance to do it for you. This does not mean you should return to a union that cannot work because the same issues that destroyed it still exist, but it does give each person a chance to reconsider what they did to bring the divorce to pass and to make the needed changes if they discover they still want to be married. For some people, this can take some time for it to sink in, and only the Holy Spirit knows who will be willing to do what it takes to change. I would encourage you to give God an opportunity to restore, and while that time period is going on, seek God's will for your life and future. I have observed that people who move on too quickly usually regret it for many different reasons.

4) To rediscover who God is in your life.

After a Christian divorces, they will want to find out what God thinks about it and how He wants them to proceed. What role will you allow God to play in your life? Will you trust God to meet your financial and emotional needs? Or, is everything hinged upon your ability to make things work? This will be a great challenge if you only trust in your ability to fix things.

Your divorce will make you feel weak, and your weakness gives God a chance to show Himself strong in your life.

5) To give yourself a chance to heal.

A person needs to heal from a divorce if for no other reason than to keep you from making the next person pay for what the last person did to you. I was so damaged, and it showed up when I least expected it to. Someone would be rude or raise their voice, and I instantly reacted. No grace here. If I saw a person mistreating another person the way I thought I had been harmed…. well, I couldn't be sure what I would do. Anyway, you get the point. I needed kindness, patience, and gentleness, combined with small amounts of truth given to me by people who loved me. Then, I had to forgive and let go, which are each necessary for the healing process to be lasting. I knew I needed to be alone to go through this process even though part of me wanted to skip it to get to the good stuff faster. But inside I knew my damage had the potential to ruin any good thing coming my way, so I stayed solo in order to heal and because God said so.

6) And finally, to rediscover who you are.

We identify so much with our roles in life, so when my role as wife and full-time mom ended, I had to figure out who I was and who I wanted to become. Fifty-four years old and having to re-define myself …. not a good place to be. Or, maybe it was?

Divorce can be an opportunity to have a do-over. To

get things right. This is not an overnight occurrence because you must first identify what wrong choices made, or participated in, that took you down a wrong path. However, while you are going through reflecting, you can also take steps to have a better future.

Chapter 10
Eilish's Story

I met Eilish at the church we both attend. She's a pretty woman with lots of spunk. As I got to know her, she would share with me some of her story, and I asked if I could share it because I know it will inspire you to put your hope in God no matter how painful your situation might be.

Eilish says, "I am writing my story because I hope it will help and encourage another woman who is single or married and in an abusive relationship. I want to assure you there is hope!"

Early on, my ability to pick the right man was broken because I did not know what a healthy relationship looked like as I had I been subjected to abuse and alcoholism growing up. With that background, I would always end up being with men who were abusive and emotionally unavailable.

In my heart, I knew there was more to a relationship than abuse, drinking, sex, and the endless cycle of wanting to be loved and accepted unconditionally but never finding it. Seeking answers, I turned to Jesus. As I started my journey with God, I found myself learning to like, and maybe even love the woman God created me to be. I believed God saw good in this broken woman.

Zephaniah 3:17, *"The Lord your God is with you. He is like a powerful soldier. He will save you. He will show how much he loves you and how happy he is with you. He will laugh and be happy*

DIVORCED YET NOT FORSAKEN

about you." Wow! Have you ever had anyone rejoice over you because you're YOU?! I never have. I've been beaten down most of my life, but God showed up and stole my heart and soul. Now, Jesus was my first love.

Still broken, I found myself starting to drift away from my new love before I gave my new faith a chance to bring about lasting change and healing in me. It was during this drifting period that I met another "man of my dreams" Tim, (not his real name) who turned into my nightmare. Tim said he had also found this redeeming love through Jesus, so how perfect was that? Within a few months of dinners, gifts, and flowers, I fell in love, and he knew he had me! I fell hook line and sinker for this handsome and seemingly kind man.

Even though I stopped reading my Bible and hanging out with my Christian friends, I still wanted God's will for my life even though I knew in my heart that I was going my own way instead of His. It wasn't long before I realized I was in another bad abusive situation.

After several attempts of breaking up with Tim, I would always go back to him, and eventually, I became pregnant. We decided to get married, and that is when the beatings started, so I kept calling off the wedding but never left the relationship and kept getting pregnant. Now I had three babies depending on me.

I never married Tim because his abuse was so severe, but what was I to do as a single mom with no income? I convinced myself I had no other choice but to endure the beatings and verbal abuse. Tim agreed to go to counseling with me, but after the fourth session, he said he was no longer interested in taking steps to make our relationship work. Our counselor advised me to run from him and never look back!

I started rereading my Bible and went back to church. There I found so much love and acceptance from God's people. I made close friends with the woman of my church who became very protective over my children and me. I was praying for God to give me the strength and wisdom to know how and when to leave Tim, and God made a way where there seemed to be no way.

At the time, I had no job or income and no education to get a good job. All I knew how to do was serving tables, but Tim didn't allow me to work, so I would have to be dependent on him for everything. He wanted complete control over me, and he did this by withholding money from me even when I needed it to buy food for our children.

Tim was not only abusive to me, but he would also yell and frightened our kids. I remember our baby was crying, and I could see something snapped in him. He started to go towards our little girl screaming for her to shut up! I ran into the room and grabbed my baby and held her close. I knew it was not safe for any of us to be there.

I had taken money from a jar that Tim kept his money in so I could buy some needed items for the kids. When he discovered I had taken his money, he questioned me about it. Scared, I denied it. Not believing me, Tim punched me on the side of my head, and I went down. Grabbing me by my hair, he pulled me back up. Right then, I knew I had to get my children and myself out! I was really in a corner, but I did have my own car, and I made my plan.

As soon as Tim left to do some side work, I grabbed a bag of clothes and diapers, put my kids in the car, and got out of there. I called my sister and asked if I could stay with her, and she said yes. My church rented a moving van, and six big men from church came and moved all my belongings out of Tim's house and put them into a rented storage unit until I got my own place.

Psalm 50:15 says, *"Call on me in the day of trouble, and I will rescue you, and you will praise me."* I was so thankful to God for delivering me from my abuser. I was also grateful to my church and sister and all the kind men who moved my belongings, and I went forward believing that God had a plan for me.

Ephesians 3:20 *"Now to Him who is able to do exceedingly abundantly above all that we ask or think, according to the power that works in us, to Him be the glory to all generations In Christ Jesus."* Yes, God's ways are higher than I can even think! He knew what He was doing and loved me right where I was. Even in my disobedience, He rescued me!

Within a week at my sister's house, things started going haywire. Little did I know she was having difficulty in her own marriage. That combined with all of us living in cramped spaces stressed us both out. Angry, she told me to leave, but I had nowhere to go. I put my kids in the car and drove to my parents to at least feed and bathe them. My parents lived in a one-bedroom apartment, so we could not stay there for long.

While I was seeking God about what to do, I felt the Lord say to my heart, "go to the subsidized apartments" around the corner from my parents. So, I drove over to the subsidized apartments, went into the office, and submitted my application. The office secretary advised me there would be a 2-year wait for a 3-bedroom apartment and I would have to take a studio apartment instead if it was available.

It was the government's rules not to put boys and girls together in the same bedroom. This rule put me at the very bottom of the list for an apartment as I had two boys and one girl. Things were really looking hopeless. By faith, I told the office secretary that I believed the Lord had instructed me to apply for these apartments, and I trusted Him to help me because He loved my babies and me. I could tell she thought I was a nut job, but within two days I was asked to come to the apartment office because she had some good news for me.

As I entered the office, the secretary looked at me in disbelief and said, "I don't know how this happened, but we have a 3-bedroom apartment available tomorrow for some strange reason, I looked at my list, and your name is at the top of the list. I don't know who you pray to, but your prayers were answered!" See how the Lord works? What an amazing witness this was to her and as far as I know, she is serving the Lord to this day.

After getting settled in our new home, I wanted to go back to school so I could provide for my family. My wonderful church paid my tuition to get my C.N.A degree, and after three months of school, I received my certificate for nursing assistant. I started working at an in-home health care business and loved my job. I was even allowed to bring my kids to work with me occasionally to cut down on babysitters. Life was not easy with raising children, paying bills, attending school activities, going to doctors, dentists, keeping gas in my car, but God was always there. I didn't have everything I wanted, but God always provided what we needed.

After I was paid on Friday, I budgeted my income and always made sure to give my tithe to the church. It never ceased to amaze me how God made sure we had our needs met even though on paper, it didn't add up.

As my faith grew, the Lord allowed me to go through some growing trials to increase my faith in Him. One Friday, when I was paying bills, I found myself left with $10 to provide food for the week. As I was holding the $10 in my hand, I started to cry and said." Lord, how is this small amount of money going to buy the food I need to feed my children for a week?"

I went into my room, fell to my knees, and cried out to God quoting His word. "Father, your word says you are the husband to the widow and the father to the fatherless. Your word says you will supply all our needs. Please, Father, show me what to do." I heard the Lord speak to my heart to take the $10 and put it in the church's offering box. He promised He would give it back to me ten-fold. I quickly did the math, and that meant He would give me back $100!

Not sure if I could believe what I just heard, I asked, "But Lord, how do I know this is not just my own brain talking?" Again, I heard, "Eilish, do you trust me?" I responded, "Yes, Lord, I do trust you, but what if I'm wrong? If I keep the $10, I can go to the store and buy some bread and peanut butter, jelly, eggs and a box of cereal. If I put it in the offering, I'm taking a chance of not having anything to feed my kids." Yet again, I heard the Lord speak to my heart, "Eilish, do you trust me?" Again, I said, "Yes, Lord, I do trust YOU!" The Lord spoke to me and said, "You and your children will witness my faithfulness."

After I decided to give my last $10 to the church, I put my kids into the car and went to do just that. Just as I was dropping my $10 into the offering box, the secretary poked her head around the corner and with amazement said, "Eilish! Someone dropped off this envelope for you about 30 minutes ago!" My kids and I were excited to open the envelope, and there it was, just as God promised me, $100, the ten-fold.

What God has done for me; he will do for you. Trust Him because He is faithful and loves you more than you know.

Chapter 11
A Time to Reflect

My Reflection Discovery

During my reflecting stage, I read a book written by Danny Silk called, "Keep Your Love On" and discovered that I had been acting like a powerless person in my marriage. I yelled and screamed to set boundaries but never really enforced them, so nothing ever changed. Part of my confusion stemmed from my Christian belief system. Wasn't a good wife supposed to submit to her husband and influence him through her quiet and gentle spirit? I didn't come close to feeling quiet or gentle, and my anger only increased because I could never figure out how to set and then enforce personal boundaries when my husband refused to respect them. And even though we had gone to many different Christian counseling sessions, nothing ever seemed to work.

At some point, I read a book written by a Christian psychologist whose opinion was that Christian counseling for marriages failed to work when they failed to make it their goal to end up with a solution that would be good for both the husband as well as the wife. The truth is, if it's not, it won't work for very long. Because of this, he saw just as many divorces in the Church as he saw outside the Church. This is not to say that I, in any way, do not hold to what the Scriptures teach, but sometimes we teach the Law and forget the spirit of the Word. After all, isn't love more excellent than all?

What went wrong and how did I contribute to it?

Why is this question important? It's not to place blame on yourself or your ex or to make you feel bad about yourself, but if you hope to have a future marriage or any healthy future relationship, then this question needs to be answered to the best of your ability because history can and does tend to repeat itself.

To answer this question of what went wrong, you might have to look for the answer outside of yourself because sometimes we just cannot see our own issues. So, maybe you are like me and cannot afford to go to a professional counselor. Don't be discouraged, because there are churches who host Divorce Care groups and several online resources, books, and inspirational speakers that you can access for free. I love, love, love! YouTube for this. I have discovered that you can learn anything you want to learn on YouTube!

For the last two years, I have listened to an inspirational speaker a day to help me move forward. In that process, I would hear these speakers talk about issues I had, but never knew I had them until I heard them described. As I was listening to them, I would think, "That's just what I did" or, that's just what I thought" and whenever I heard something that applied to me, I took note and researched it further.

In this chapter, I discuss several personalities and behavioral issues that could be considerations for what went wrong in your marriage. As we go through these, you may see yourself or your ex-having these issues.

Either way, you would be wise to pay attention either to fix them in yourselves or to look for them in any future relationships you may want to go into.

Relationship Boundaries

So, what is a relationship boundary? Setting a relationship boundary is saying the word no to requests asked of you that are not in your best interest. For example, requests like, "Can you cover for me at work this weekend," or, "Can you take off work so you can take me to the airport?", or "Could you babysit my child for free so I can work?" If you are a people pleaser or if you are afraid of conflict, you will have a hard time saying no. However, if you don't learn how to say no to requests that are not in your best interest, you will suffer.

Saying no in a marriage can be especially tricky because we can and should want to please our spouses. But our spouses can sometimes be selfish, controlling, or even abusive, and that's when you will need to risk making them angry by saying, "No, I'm unable to do that." It's when you decide to both set and stick to your "no" decisions, that you have a chance at getting your best interests back into play. The bottom line is if you fail to make decisions for yourself, it does you no good to blame another for your failure to take care of yourself. After all, they are making their decisions motivated by their self-interests.

The Fixer

Another person who will find themselves repeatedly

overstepping another person's boundaries is the "fixer." This is the person who can't stand to see a situation that is broken. They will either tell you how to fix it or they will step in to save the day by fixing it themselves. How did they cross a boundary line? They took over another person's responsibilities. For example: I refuse to mow my neighbor's lawn no matter how tall his grass gets, and he does not mow my lawn. His lawn is his responsibility, and my lawn is mine. A fixer will find themselves doing everything for the people around them. Not surprisingly, the people around them will be happy that they no longer have to mow their lawns anymore. In fact, they may say to you, "If you don't like seeing how tall my grass has gotten, then you mow it. It's your problem, not mine." You get the point?

I know this sounds a little bit ridiculous, but that describes what most of us are doing. Mothers who do everything for their children. Or, husbands who feel they are doing it all while their wives do nothing at home. Both may get irritated, but they continue to do it all for their own reasons. They may feel trapped in the situation of their own making and can't figure out how to change it. They ask and ask and ask for the people in their family to contribute, but their family members have all discovered that you will do it if they don't. When this has gone on for a long while it will be near impossible to reverse it without taking drastic measures, and that is when talk of divorce starts to take place.

But what if everyone had understood whose responsibility was whose and insisted on everyone doing what they were supposed to do from the beginning?

Fewer divorces and maybe fewer future divorces would occur.

A fixer might have to let things stay broken to reset broken boundaries, but never compromise their principles by supporting another person's bad behaviors that they are joined to. In other words, if you don't say no to your spouse's spending habits and can't find a way to separate yourself from the debts they make, then their debt will end up being your debt too.

The truth be told, whenever you fail or are unable to take actions to stop another person's bad choices from affecting you, then in effect their choices will become your choices, and you will experience their consequences.

Co-dependency

A co-dependent person is a people pleaser. They work hard to please others wanting to gain their approval so they can feel good about themselves. They lack self-confidence apart from other people telling them they are right. Co-dependents will make many personal sacrifices just to please their loved ones even when they don't get the same back.

There are different degrees of this, and you will have to decide where you fall into this syndrome. I know for myself that I love to give to others. I wanted to make my loved ones lives easier and was their biggest cheerleader. But when I didn't get the same back from them, or their gratitude, I hit the pause button. It was then the Lord spoke to my heart. He said, "Giving people can produce spoiled people." After I heard His words, I took a good look at how my actions had been affecting the people I had been giving to. I had thought that my example of giving would inspire them to become givers too, but it didn't seem like it was working. Then I felt the Lord said I needed to teach by example and by giving them opportunities to give back. I would know how successful my training methods were by their willingness to give to another even when it cost them something.

A Co-Dependent's Need for Validation

We all want to be heard and listened to without others judging us. It would be great if instead of judging us, they even agreed with us. No man is an island. We were created for fellowship, and the quality of our relationships will include other people approving of us, especially the people closest to us, but when we don't get their approval, and we shut down because of the disapproval, that is where the problem comes in. They may have disapproved of us for their own reasons. Reasons they may not even be aware that they possess. This is when a healthy person will believe in themselves and follow what they know to be right rather that sub-coming to outside pressures siding against them.

If you don't follow your personal belief system, you will find that you have given control of your life over to another person who may not have your best interests in mind. In the end, the person I need approval from is God and myself. I need to live an authentic, honest life that I can be proud of and a life that has a purpose.

Narcissistic Tendencies

As I said, I hate to put labels on any person, but if you see yourself or another with some of all of the following characteristics, it might give you some insight on how to change or who to avoid. If it does not apply to you, then move on. As I studied this, I thought to myself, this sounds like another word for pride and selfishness, which we all possess on some level.

A person who is a narcissist will have an over-inflated view of themselves. They believe themselves to be better than others and will work to be the center of attention craving admiration from others. They can be charming in public but mean in private. They are self-centered and self-absorbed even though they may suffer from low self-esteem. Narcissists can see themselves as victims, especially when they receive any form of criticisms. They will perceive all criticisms as a put down instead of help.

Many times, these people are not happy, but because they fight to protect their image, they will find it impossible to show themselves as less than they believe themselves to be. But the good news is if you see you have been acting like this, you can change! But it will require humility, and there is the conflict.

A narcissist can be extremely difficult to be in a relationship with because they will fight for control and will put you down so they can feel better about themselves. They usually have only their interests in

113

mind, so they lack empathy for what you are experiencing due to their treatment of you. It will always be your fault and never theirs. They can also lie to themselves because they desperately need to believe they are a good person and any truth that would come into conflict with that must be wrong.

A relationship with this person will require that you have good self-esteem, be long-suffering, and possess great patience. Most people lose their self-confidence living with a narcissist and must escape to save themselves. Love does cover a multitude of sins and a co-dependent person who lacks confidence may find themselves trapped by indecisiveness, making it almost impossible to escape.

Gaslighting

This is when a person will try to make you question your reality so they can continue to do what they are doing. They may say to you, "You're too sensitive." Or, "That's not how that happened," when you know it did happen that way. They will work to get you to question yourself to control the situation to their advantage. These people will mess with your head. The best thing to do is to find a safe person to talk to who can help you see things clearly.

Passive Aggressive

These are people who don't know how to deal with their emotions during a relationship conflict, so they shut down. Responses like "I'm fine," Or "Whatever," during a conversation followed by their silent treatment will let you know that they are not okay. This is not to be confused with taking a time out from a heated conversation so you can regain emotional control intending to return to talk again.

Another passive aggressive behavior could be a "dig" or a "put down" during a conversation that also lets you know this person has something against you. Sometimes passive-aggressive people will use behaviors like the silent treatment to punish the person they are offended with.

Controlling People

People who try to control other people will use weapons like anger, shame, or guilt to pressure and manipulate you into doing what they believe is right. A better way to convince you would be if they gave you their honest opinion as to what they thought was right and then leave it with you to make your own decision. It could be that they are trying to control you because they fear they will experience consequences from your actions. Even so, if you feel another person is controlling you, you will have to establish clear boundaries to stop it.

Explosive People

Walking around your house like you are walking on eggshells in fear that at the least provocation the person you live with is going to have a meltdown and then later blame it on you for causing their meltdown is no way to live. "If you hadn't done this" or "if you hadn't said that" are all perfect justifications for their fits of anger. Sometimes their anger will be displayed through a verbal assault, including name-calling, and sometimes it will include physical violence. Their short fuses could be the result of a lack of discipline during their childhood years.

Addictive Behaviors

People who have food, drug, alcohol, video games, gambling, shopping, or pornography addictions bring added stress to their relationships and marriages. The bad news is there is no quick fix. The good news is, there is a fix, but it could take years of going through the process. But if you don't quit, you can be changed. *"For sin shall no longer be your master, because you are not under the law, but under grace."* (Romans 6:14)

It starts with wanting to change. Then you will need to take actions towards changing, perhaps by joining a support group that offers accountability and mentoring. You will also need to adjust your expectations to allow for failures (which everyone has), and that is when a mentor or support group becomes so valuable. They will encourage you to start over again. They have already been where you are and know that the secret to overcoming is not quitting.

The phrase *"practice makes perfect"* really applies to getting set free from addictions. When a person first starts to learn a new behavior, they won't be very good at it. It's as they continue to practice that behavior that they will master it. *"I have the right to do anything"*—but I will not be mastered by anything." (1 Corinthians 6:12)

Finding a mentor who is willing to speak the truth to you in love is also essential because it is the truth that will set you free. A person who has addictions should always believe it is God's will for them to be set free even though they may have to go through a long process to get free.

Once you have learned how to overcome your addiction, then becoming a mentor will be an important next step to your personal growth. Teaching someone else what you just learned will strengthen your commitment to stay addiction free. It's when we give back to another person in need, that we receive more of what we need.

Enablers

Enablers are fixers that prevent their loved ones from experiencing consequences that would cause them to change. They can be parents or spouses who keep bailing their family members out of the messes they create. For example, an enabler may tell someone that they are done bailing them out from jail, but when their loved one calls crying, they run to the rescue and bail them out. Or, they may scream that you need to get a job but continue to support you when you don't.

Enablers communicate to the people they help that they have stopped believing in them. They just don't think their loved one could make it without their help, so they continue to cover for them … and the beat goes on.

Enabling doesn't happen overnight but increases as the

enabler trains their loved ones to expect their help each and every time that they cry for it. The only way to fix it is to not fix it. There comes a time when the enabler will actually have to enforce the boundaries that they said they were setting. I am never going to bail you out from jail again and then refuse to bail your loved one out no matter how threatening they become.

Enablers must realize that all their help has failed to fix anything and that they now need to be fixed. Only when they stop helping their loved ones, forcing them to take responsibility for their wrong choices, will there ever be any real chance for change.

This brings us to how a person's self-image will determine their response to the bad behaviors I just listed. Why do we allow people to abuse and mistreat us? Do we think we are not worthy of respect? Or, do we not believe the person treating us so disrespectfully loves us enough to change the way they are treating us if we threaten to end the relationship for refusing to change? Do we think we can't do any better?

Would we ever allow anybody to abuse our children in these ways? Even so, do we believe God would want others to abuse and mistreat His children? I understand that at times, we have to exercise patience and long-suffering in some relationships. God shows us patience and long-suffering too. But then there comes a time when those same good qualities become enablers keeping people in their bad behaviors. This is the tricky part. How to decide what to do and when. This is also where our relationship with the Holy Spirit becomes so important. Only He knows if or when a person is ready to change or when a person needs to depart. Humans are messy, and love is necessary to walk with some people.

Where Do You See Yourself in This Chapter?

I want to end this chapter by asking the same question I asked at the beginning of this chapter. What went wrong, and how did I contribute? Maybe you read something in this chapter that did apply to you. Hopefully, you will take the time to work on changing yourself in the days to come so you can have the future you always dreamed of. It's still possible and may be more satisfying than you could have imagined.

Chapter 12
Disappointments and Regrets

Pursuing a dream with all your heart, only to have it ripped away from you, will leave you in a very dark place. One thing I have noticed in my 64 years is that disappointments come to us all. Life just happens. However, there are some failures that we caused, and that is when regrets will come. Knowing that it was your choices that caused your dream to crash. What do you do with that? In some cases, you will be filled with regrets without knowing of any solutions. You just can't figure out how to undo the damage you've done.

I can only imagine the regrets people experience on their death bed. They look back at their life and don't like what they see and now have no way to change anything. The dye has been cast, and it is what it is. Maybe they were too proud to admit what they did wrong or to ask for forgiveness. Their need to be right, took away another person's desire to be heard and a multitude of hurts later, their victims cannot find it in them to forgive, even though they now are no longer too proud to ask for it. I wonder what advice they would give to another person to help them avoid where they find themselves? I would guess that they would advise you to humble yourself sooner rather than later and before it is too late.

Psalm 27:13 says, *"I would have despaired unless I had believed I would see the goodness of the Lord in the Land of the living"* (NIV) How true this was for me. I would sit on the edge of despair year after year watching my hopes and dreams slipping away, fighting to keep hold of them only to see them disappear in spite of my efforts, leaving me to wonder why I should ever try again. Why indeed?

This dark night of the soul can go on for years, and unless you grab on to hope, you could die there never having seen anything more come from your life here on earth. We only get one life. It is a gift from God. There must be something more important than ourselves, a bigger picture that we must see to motivate us to get off the couch and to live life again.

Fail Forward

I love the advice singer Johnny Cash gives in this quote: "You build on failure. You use it as a steppingstone. Close the door on the past. You don't try to forget the mistakes, but you don't dwell on it. You don't let it have any of your energy, or any of your time, or any of your space."

You Must Forget Your Past to Go Forward.

I have seen people who are so broken by their past experiences that they find themselves unable to move forward. They become sad people. *"Brothers and sisters, I do not consider myself yet to have taken hold of it. But one thing I do: Forgetting what is behind and straining toward what is ahead."* (Phil.3:13) If your past has traumatized you, you must also choose to forget your past to have a future. You cannot live in both places. My past wanted me to stay in it. It wanted to keep me depressed and sad. If I gave in to it, I would have no future worth having. I had to decide to go forward depressed but still go forward. I had to believe that I would once again, *"see the goodness of the Lord in the land of the living,"* (Psalm 27:13)

Part of dealing with our failures is to ask forgiveness and to make restitution if it is the right thing to do. Walking away without making things right is not really the answer. But you can only do what you can do, then go forward determined to do better. Don't allow your life to be defined by your failures. There are too many examples of successful people who failed over and over again but who also refused to quit, and they went on to do amazing things. Thomas A. Edison said, "I have not failed. I've just found 10,000 ways that won't work."

I refuse to live a life without purpose, no matter how difficult or painful. There must be more than just this present-day life, and there has to be more than little old me to care about. I don't know what will motivate you to move forward once again, but for me, it was my faith in Jesus and his promise that I would once again see the goodness of the Lord in the land of the living.

The Lord spoke to my heart saying, "You don't know what is at stake here. If you did, you would be willing to pay the price of suffering if needed to accomplish what I created you for. Others need your gifts and talents. They need your experience to help them in their life. They need to see your example of how to be an over-comer for the day will come to them when they also need to overcome. They need to see an example of a person rising from the ashes of defeat to live their best life. Your children also need to see what faith can do in your life. They need to see you keep trying and not to give up. I went forward, trusting God to give me beauty in exchange for my ashes and He has.

Chapter 13
A Time to Build Again

Alongside the reflecting and healing period, a person should also take positive steps towards a better future. Progressing in life is so vital to maintaining happiness. Each of us had an idea of what we wanted our lives to look like and when we experience a divorce, we are left to figure out how to get back to how we dreamed our lives would look like or if that could ever happen again.

To Begin: Start to imagine what your new life could look like. Every dream starts with a vision. You must see it in your mind before you go for it. Remember that life is not over, just different, and you have a chance to redefine your life to be what you want it to be.

Find a mentor or an example of a success story to follow. I remember thinking about a woman I knew who had been divorced with five children. When I met her, she was a successful businesswoman who owned a beautiful home. Her children all adored her and were all living successful lives. I used to wonder how she did it. Then. when my divorce happened, she became my example to follow. If God did it for her, He would do it for me. I knew I would have to risk take and be brave as I went forward alone, but I wanted to see better days. I did not want to see my life end in destruction.

You Must Leave Your Comfort Zone

Start to view life as an adventure waiting for you to show up to discover it. But to go on this adventure, you must decide to leave your comfort zone. This will seem like risk-taking for a while until you get past the beginning stages, there is no other way to get to the good stuff. As you begin to get out of your comfort zone to re-discover who you are again without your ex, you will realize that you have a chance at a life do-over. This was hard for me because I was 54 years old at the time of my divorce, so I wasn't sure if I had any youthful optimism or ambition left in me that could motivate me enough to want to start over again.

I was wondering if my best years were over or whether I even desired to go for it again. It seems I had lost some of my identity and maybe even my purpose. But sometimes new doors of opportunity can only come when old doors close and so it was with me. My life as I knew it had ended, and that caused me to look for another one, which led me to find more of what God had for me. Could it be that my greatest years of purpose and personal fulfillment were ahead of me?

I had heard of people achieving great things in their later years like Colonel Sanders, who started his first franchised Kentucky Fried Chicken store when he was 65 years old. Who does that at that age? It boggled my mind to think of doing something like that.

At the same time, my age was speaking to me in another way that did end up motivating me into action. I only had so many years left to do something for the Lord and for others. I knew in my heart that I wanted to leave my mark by somehow making this earth a better place before I died. I did not want to appear before Jesus knowing I had not gone forward because of some defeats and had decided to have a pity party instead.

Renewing My Mind

Surprisingly, this time of loss caused me to re-evaluate my life and think about how I wanted it to end up. In the beginning, it seemed like my life had been burned up, similar to the loss a person experiences after their home has burned to the ground, and they gratefully escape with their lives. Their loss helped them to see what was really important. That's what my loss was causing me to see. The Lord revealed to me that my life was not over but was merely being readjusted by Him to bring forth greater fruit. As I thought about it, I realized I had a chance to rebuild my life using the wisdom I had gained from my past. You really need to be this positive. It's hard to start over, but I'm glad I did. It has taken time to rebuild, but I am now enjoying the fruit of my labor.

To get this future, you must stop looking at your loss, and choose instead to look at all the potential your future holds. My age was my biggest hindrance. I wondered if I was too old to start over again, but I had to re-adjust my thinking. To do so, I started to watch inspirational speakers on YouTube daily. I knew I had to overcome my negativity and work to renew my mind if I was going to experience the good life I desired. I plan to continue watching these speakers because I will always need to be encouraged and challenged to do better if I am going to live my best life.

Divorce can be a great opportunity to reclaim your

life. As I write this book, I have to wonder what happened to my sense of adventure? Why do I have fear now instead of excitement? That's not who I am. I am a dreamer. I love to dance, play in the rivers, create new businesses, meet new people. My favorite age was my early 20s when life was before me just waiting for me to discover it. That girl still exists in some form, and I want to get back to her because I had a lot more fun being her than who I am now.

I had to look at my future with new eyes. I had to readjust my dreams of how I envisioned my life would look like and even though my future goals are now different, I really like where I am going. I came to realize that my divorce gave me a chance to rediscover who I was and to develop more of my God-given gifts and talents.

Actions you can take to start reclaiming your life: To begin, start to do the things again that you used to love doing. Taking vacations, bike riding, cooking, taking walks, seeing movies, re-connecting with old friends, reading books. Get back to some of who you were before by doing some of the things you used to do.

Take an exercise class or join a gym. People tend to feel better about themselves when they think they look better. Working out will give you the feeling that you are reclaiming your life. It will also provide you with something to do with all the free time you now have and into a social environment without social expectations.

Start to invest in your future earning potential by taking

a class to improve your work skills or just for interest. Some very inexpensive online courses teach every software there is by some of the best teachers in the world. I love to learn this way as it meets my financial means and my time constraints. Lynda.com and skillshare.com are two of my favorites. Maybe you've always wanted to learn how to cook Italian or Chinese food. Then you could feed your friends with a meal using your new skills. After a divorce is a great time to learn new things.

There are meet up groups located in most of the larger cities that organize groups according to interests. This helps you meet people who are interested in doing activities you are interested in. These groups were created for people who don't know anyone in the group the first time they attend. They were designed to connect strangers with the same interests.

Find a place to volunteer. I love volunteers because they are giving people. This is one of the things I did after my divorce, and I was able to meet some wonderful people.

Chapter 14
Biblical Considerations

So, when is it time to think about dating or getting remarried? A Christian should answer this question by searching the scriptures to find out what God would have them do, and that's where I want to start this chapter.

God Always Works to Redeem Men and Women.

From the time of Adam and Eve, men and women have disobeyed God's commandments and needed redemption. Throughout our lifetime, we will find ourselves missing the mark of God's standards. Divorce is another failure of man to live up to God's standards and with every failure, God works to redeem and restore a person when they turn back to God in humble repentance. *"May God himself, the God of peace, sanctify you through and through. May your whole spirit, soul and body be kept blameless at the coming of our Lord Jesus Christ. The one who calls you is faithful, and he will do it."* (1 Thessalonians 5:23-24)

Divorce is not the one sin that God refuses to redeem. God's love covers a multitude of sins and will look for ways to bring a sinner back into fellowship with Him. Jesus said, *"I desire mercy, not sacrifice. For I have not come to call the righteous, but sinners."* (Matthew 9:13)

At the same time, we should never take His redemptive work for granted and use it as a license to sin. That path leads to destruction. However, at the end of all that destruction, when a person turns to God again, He will work to redeem their relationship with Him and restore their purpose. It's what God does, and it is who He is.

The Difficulties of Marriage

2 Timothy 3:1-7 warns the Church about the character issues men and women would display in the last days. I believe this will make marriage very difficult as we approach those days.

"But mark this: There will be terrible times in the last days. People will be lovers of themselves, lovers of money, boastful, proud, abusive, disobedient to their parents, ungrateful, unholy, without love, unforgiving, slanderous, without self-control, brutal, not lovers of the good, treacherous, rash, conceited, lovers of pleasure rather than lovers of God— having a form of godliness but denying its power. Have nothing to do with such people.

They are the kind who worm their way into homes and gain control over gullible women, who are loaded down with sins and are swayed by all kinds of evil desires, always learning but never able to come to a knowledge of the truth.

What Did Jesus Say about Divorce and Remarriage?

"Some Pharisees came to him to test him. They asked, 'Is it lawful for a man to divorce his wife for any and every reason?'"

"Haven't you read," he replied, "that at the beginning the Creator 'made them male and female,' and said, 'For this reason a man will leave his father and mother and be united to his wife, and the two will become one flesh' So they are no longer two, but one flesh.

Therefore what God has joined together, let no one separate."

"Why then," they asked, "did Moses command that a man give his wife a certificate of divorce and send her away?"

Jesus replied, "Moses permitted you to divorce your wives because your hearts were hard. But it was not this way from the beginning. I tell you that anyone who divorces his wife, except for sexual immorality, and marries another woman commits adultery."

The disciples said to him, "If this is the situation between a husband and wife, it is better not to marry."

Jesus replied, "Not everyone can accept this word, but only those to whom it has been given. For there are eunuchs who were born that way, and there are eunuchs who have been made eunuchs by others—and there are those who choose to live like eunuchs for the sake of the kingdom of heaven. The one who can accept this should accept it." (Matthew 19:3-12).

God created marriage for the benefit of man. Life can get hard, and it is a comfort to share both the burdens and the joys of being with another person. Even so, God allowed men to divorce their wives in the Old Testament because their hearts were hard. Divorce, for this reason, was a mercy permitted by God. Otherwise, a woman would be subjected to an abusive marriage where her husband could continue to mistreat her.

Every time I read the above scripture, I think to myself, "men and women's hearts are still hard." Therefore, I believe God continues to allow divorce for the same reason He allowed it in Moses' time even though it was never His will for man. We may have grace available to us today, but that doesn't mean we are employing it to live godly lives.

What I find surprising from this scripture is the response of the disciples after hearing Jesus' words. When they heard they could not be divorced for any reason, they decided it was better not to marry at all. When they voiced their concerns to Jesus, He told them that their other option was to be a eunuch. In other words, a life without sex apart from a marriage covenant. Sadly, it seems that divorce was commonplace in their culture.

God Divorced Israel

In the book of Jeremiah 3:8, God, *"gave faithless Israel her certificate of divorce and sent her away because of all her adulteries."* God divorced Israel because she had committed spiritual adultery by worshiping other gods. I had never thought about God divorcing until a preacher pointed this scripture text out. God hates divorce but refused to be married to Israel when they repeatedly were unfaithful to Him.

Paul's Teaching on Divorce and Remarriage

"Now to the unmarried[a] and the widows I say: It is good for them to stay unmarried, as I do. But if they cannot control themselves, they should marry, for it is better to marry than to burn with passion.

To the married I give this command (not I, but the Lord): A wife must not separate from her husband. But if she does, she must remain unmarried or else be reconciled to her husband. And a husband must not divorce his wife.

To the rest I say this (I, not the Lord): If any brother has a wife who is not a believer and she is willing to live with him, he must not divorce her. And if a woman has a husband who is not a believer and he is willing to live with her, she must not divorce him. For the unbelieving husband has been sanctified through his wife, and the unbelieving wife has been sanctified through her believing husband. Otherwise your children would be unclean, but as it is, they are holy.

But if the unbeliever leaves, let it be so. The brother or the sister is not bound in such circumstances; God has called us to live in peace." (1 Corinthians 7: 8-15).

If a man or a woman cannot control their sexual passions, Paul advises them to marry. His advice brings me back to Jesus' words that not everyone could receive His teachings on divorce and remarriage. God created men and women to possess sexual desires, but they should not be fulfilled outside of a marriage covenant. I would exhort you to honor God with your bodies and to prayerfully seek God's will in all your marriage, divorce and remarriage decisions.

Marrying an unbeliever will cause conflict in a marriage and we are told not to do it for those reasons. But there are occasions when a person decides to become a Christ follower after they were married and, in these cases, Paul gives them his advice to allow an unbelieving spouse to leave the marriage.

Seeking Wise Counsel

God has placed Pastors and other religious leaders to be spiritual authorities over the body of Christ. Part of their job is to warn a person when they see them going in the wrong direction. Therefore, for our own safety, we should seek their advice, especially when it comes to marriage, divorce, and re-marriage. I highly value the spiritual authorities in my life and carefully listen to their words as they pray for me. So many times, I will hear the voice of the Lord speak through them to me.

I won't tell another person what they should do. It is for them to seek God's will for themselves. I would only advise that a person seek their pastors' counsel, obey their conscience and do what they truly believe the Holy Spirit and Scripture teach Because, in the end, we must all give an account to God alone for the choices we make in life.

Chapter 15
A Time to Dream Again

Carol's Story

After I had been attending Divorce Care for a while, I started to feel better and felt like I wanted to meet new people and maybe even go out on a date. My good friend knew I was considering dating, and she gave me some of her best advice. She counseled me that I was not healthy enough to date and would not be for a long time. Affirming me she said, nobody could be after what I went through for 26 years. It was hard to hear, but inside I knew she was right. She made me promise not to date anyone until I was healthy again because the odds were, I would only attract unhealthy people and repeat the same mistake again.

I took her words to heart and readjusted my plans. My first goal from then on was to be there for my children first and foremost. Next, I wanted to find out what happened, how it happened, how I contributed to the demise of our relationship, and how NOT to pick the same person again, as the statistics said that I probably would. I wanted to heal so that when I did start a new relationship, I would not bring the old baggage with me.

Through this process, I re-discovered the girl I used to be. The girl who had been put on a shelf hidden all those years. I loved every minute of finding me again. My sister, who was divorced said she noticed things about herself in that timeframe that she had forgotten, so it was like finding yourself all over again. I found that to be true for me too.

All I can say is that taking the time to heal was the best thing I ever did. In the end, I did not date for several years, but when I was ready to date again, I met a guy through a Christian online dating service and am now super happily married after 10 years of marriage. I am so glad I took the time for myself to heal.

Just like Carol, maybe you feel it's God's will for you to remarry. The following are some practical things to consider.

Online Dating

Online dating has made it easier than ever to date again. It has become our wonderful modern-day matchmaker. Today, there are Christian online dating services that can be a handy tool to meet people who are like-minded and share your Christian values. I know several people who have successfully re-married due to using an online dating service.

Online Predators

Like it or not, there are online predators out there looking for newly divorced people because they know they will be more vulnerable. A newer divorcee's need to feel attractive, be listened to, or any other need, could cause them to be emotionally available even if the person they choose to date is not the right person for them. Sadly, if they go ahead and date a person just because they know what to say or do to attract you, but are not God's best for them, they could end up even more damaged than they already are.

Even so, don't be so fearful that you cannot go forward. Just slow the process down and be smart. When you meet a person online, it gives you a chance to talk via the online message service. This will provide you with an opportunity to get to know them or to ask them some questions that may be important to you. They will have their questions too. Then meet at a safe location and go from there. You don't have to marry the person you meet for lunch. It's just a chance for you to see if there is anything about this person that attracts you.

Today People Can Easily Hide Their Issues.

Watch the person you are dating to see how they treat their existing relationships. Pay attention to how they treat the people who wait on you in restaurants. Take the time to talk to their pastor or ask to check the history on their computer. I would. Marriage covenants are to be fearfully entered, so do what you have to do to know who you are becoming one with.

I know of three incredible women who married men and only afterward discovered their new husbands had been hiding their real life from them. One woman learned she had married a man with a drug and sex problem. Another married a man who was behind on his taxes and only discovered it because she was the first one to get the mail that day. It took them years to pay off that debt, and she felt lied to. Another woman married a man who she thought was a fellow college student only to find out he had never attended any classes. When it came time to graduate, he had a very reasonable excuse for why he couldn't attend. She was an honest, loving woman who came from an open and honest family and had no idea that anyone could live a lie, so she wasn't looking for it.

Dating from a Position of Strength

When I talk to people about what they considered when looking at someone to date (with the intentions of getting remarried), they would always mention the amount of baggage a person had from previous relationships or behaviors. For example: how much child support would they have to pay out each month, which would not be available to pay joint bills? Will the children accept the marriage, or work to make your life miserable? How much debt do they have? Do they have any addictions? How much drama does their extended family create? Do they share a belief in Christ? I could go on and on. Some of these considerations may sound selfish but may still be valid, especially if they stem from what went wrong in their previous marriage.

When you marry a person, you marry all their issues, and vice-versa. This one consideration should give anyone pause. I do understand the neediness a person experiences after a divorce but moving too quickly can take you from the frying pan into the fire. Yikes! If you think you are in a bad place now, a hasty move may be even worse.

I listed behaviors and baggage people may not want to deal with, but another question to ask is; "What baggage or behaviors do I have that I need to get rid of?" Obviously, getting rid of your kids is not the baggage I am talking about. But what about anger issues, trust issues, debt, or insecurities? See yourself through the eyes of the person you want to marry and become the person they would want to be with.

Dating with Children

Dating or getting remarried with children will have a different set of considerations, especially if your children are teenagers. They may not like the person you have chosen and will resent having them forced upon them. This could bring out extreme anger and rebellion in them. On the other hand, younger children who are not as defensive as teenagers, naturally crave affection and will form attachments to the person you are dating. They can become hurt and confused when you decide to stop dating, so be slow to introduce your children to the people you date. Problems with children are why most second marriages end in divorce. There are whole books written on this subject and for a good reason.

Wait for God's Best

"He has made everything beautiful in its time." (Ecclesiastes 3:11) There was a song I used to listen to every day. The lyrics were "In His time, in His time, The Lord makes everything beautiful, in His time." Those lyrics

repeated over and over again. The song was peaceful to listen to but also disturbing, as I thought to myself, "When God, when?"

Over the years, I remember cringing whenever I heard this Scripture because all I could hear was: WAIT! No one likes to wait for what they desire, and I was no exception. Year after year, my flesh wanted what it wanted, but God's Holy Spirit asked me to trust Him to satisfy my needs and desires daily.

It literally took me years to trust God enough not to take things into my own hands. I finally trusted God only because it never really worked out the way I wanted when I did things my own way. Now, I am seeing His wisdom and plans for me. Today, I am glad I chose to use restraint and to wait for His timing. My advice to you while you are waiting: always believe God has your best in mind and has someone He wants you to be with. This faith will keep you steady as you take the necessary time to get ready for them.

Generosity

In my opinion, the primary character quality I would look for in a mate besides being physically attracted to them, would be the quality of generosity. A generous person will always look for ways to bless their mate. Selfishness on the other hand, destroys most relationships.

Chapter 16
How to Be Financially Secure

I believe financial insecurities to be one of the top issues after a divorce – it certainly was for me. You can become financially secure in Christ as you apply His principles. However, first, you must know what they are and how to do it.

Scriptures That Promise God's Provision

The Bible is filled with Scriptures that promise God's provision. The following are a few key verses:

In Matthew 6:26, Jesus said, *"Look at the birds of the air; they do not sow or reap or store away in barns, and yet your heavenly Father feeds them. Are you not much more valuable than they?"*

Philippians 4:19, *"And my God will meet all your needs according to the riches of his glory in Christ Jesus."*

Psalm 34:9-10, *"Fear the Lord, you his holy people, for those who fear him lack nothing. The lions may grow weak and hungry, but those who seek the Lord lack no good thing."*

Psalm 37:25, *"I was young and now I am old, yet I have never seen the righteous forsaken or their children begging bread."*

Psalm 37:19, *"In times of disaster they [the righteous] will not wither; in days of famine they will enjoy plenty."*

Jehovah-Jireh Genesis 22:14, *"The Lord Will Provide."* Jehovah-Jireh is one of God's names. It was through His names that God communicated His covenant promises to the Israelites. So, when God called Himself Jehovah-Jireh, *"The Lord Will Provide,"* He was telling the Israelites that they could trust Him to provide for them.

Testing God's Promise to Provide

In Matthew 6:31-33, Jesus said, *"So do not worry, saying, 'What shall we eat?' or 'What shall we drink?' or 'What shall we wear?' For the pagans run after all these things, and your heavenly Father knows that you need them. But seek first his kingdom and his righteousness, and all these things will be given to you as well."*

I had been a Christian for about three years when I decided to find out if this Scripture was true. My husband and I had started a new business, and as with any new adventure, we had been hoping for great success. Hard times had fallen upon us, making it challenging to buy needed groceries with what was left over after paying our bills. Whenever it got tight, I would borrow money from my sister to help us get by. I was overwhelmed with financial pressures and didn't know what I could trust God for. I needed to know what God could do all by Himself without any help from me. I had put my trust in Him when we decided to start our business, and as I read this Scripture over and over again, I wondered if God really meant what He had said.

There was a condition attached to His promise of provision, which was to *"seek first His kingdom and His righteousness."* During my devotions, I had been meditating on what *"seeking first His kingdom"* could mean. It was then the Holy Spirit challenged me to pursue God's Kingdom in the same way I had been pursuing my business. His challenge stopped me cold. I knew in my heart that it was the Lord speaking to me. I also knew that I had been pursuing my business with all my heart. I realized that I could not pursue both my business and His Kingdom with the same heartfelt desire and energy. One of them would have to take second place. This is what Jesus meant when He told the disciples, *"No one can serve two masters. Either you will hate the one and love the other, or you will be devoted to the one and despise the other. You cannot serve both God and money."* (Matthew 6:24)

I decided that day to serve God, to pursue righteous living, and to prioritize His Kingdom first in my life. Now I needed to know if He would add all those other things unto me.

Memorial Day weekend came, and we were nearly out of food. We had one package of meat, two potatoes, a small bag of noodles and $1.65. To know what God could provide all by Himself, we agreed not to borrow money or tell anyone of our predicament. We took the money and bought six eggs and a quart of milk. We ate what we had on Friday night and had enough left over for breakfast on Saturday. After breakfast, we went on with our day, taking a walk, wondering how God would provide dinner for us.

We had lived in Chicago for four years and had never been invited out to eat. However, that night as we approached our apartment, our neighbor, who was out walking his dog, invited us over to dinner explaining that his wife had made a huge pot of chili and they could use our help to eat it all.

145

The next day was Sunday, and we went to church, feeling sure that God would impress someone to give us money to buy groceries. Keeping to our decision to remain silent, we went home disappointed, trying to figure out what we would eat that day. As soon as we approached our apartment, another tenant raised his window and invited us to eat with them. As it happened, his wife had also made too much food. We ate lunch and took some home at their insistence.

It was now Memorial Day. No businesses or banks would be opened that day, and again, I pondered how God would feed us. Even the cat was out of food. I remember spending an hour looking for spare change under the cushions of the couch and throughout the house before I found the 22 cents needed to buy him a can of cat food. To say the least, we were so depressed that we decided to stay in. That afternoon a client called asking if she could pick up her order apologizing for bothering us on a holiday. I agreed to meet her, expecting to be paid by check. To my surprise, she paid in cash, and I was now able to buy the groceries we needed. But more importantly, I knew God's Word was true, and I could rest trusting Him to add unto us all those things we needed.

God Promises Provision to Those who Tithe

Soon after I became a Christian, I would hear other Christians share how God would meet their needs supernaturally all because they tithed. Because of their testimonies, I also decided to tithe and discovered the same truth they had discovered.

After a divorce, many people will experience financial difficulties. To those people, I will give you the same advice I was given by others years ago to trust God by giving him ten percent of your income and watch what He will do for you.

Malachi 3:8-11

The following passage is often referred to when the subject of tithing is taught. *"Will a mere mortal rob God? Yet you rob me. But you ask, 'How are we robbing you?' In tithes and offerings. You are under a curse – your whole nation – because you are robbing me. Bring the whole tithe into the storehouse, that there may be food in my house. Test me in this," says the Lord Almighty, "and see if I will not throw open the floodgates of heaven and pour out so much blessing that there will not be room enough to store it.* ***I will prevent pests from devouring your crops,*** *and the vines in your fields will not drop their fruit before it is ripe," says the Lord Almighty.* (emphasis added).

Tithing to some seems to be a burden placed upon them by God that gives them no benefits. But this couldn't be further from the truth. Tithing, or giving God one-tenth of your income, has promises of provision, blessing, and protection attached to it.

Tithing Existed Before the Law

There are many who say tithing was eliminated when Jesus came. They say the tithe was part of the Law and we are now under the period of grace. Abraham, who is called the father of our faith, lived before Moses and the Law, and he gave God a tenth of his income, as told in Genesis 14. Therefore, tithing existed before the Law.

Jesus Didn't Eliminate the Tithe

In Matthew 23:23, Jesus said, *"Woe to you, teachers of the law and Pharisees, you hypocrites! You give a tenth of your spices – mint, dill and cumin. But you have neglected the more important matters of the law – justice, mercy and faithfulness. You should have practiced the latter, without neglecting the former."* Jesus didn't tell them to stop tithing. He told them to do all of it: tithe, show mercy, justice, and faithfulness.

This last statement points out that giving to God financially isn't a fix-all solution to your problems. There may be other areas of your life that aren't in line with the Word of God. We need to take the whole Word of God into consideration when we are following Jesus.

Cheerful Givers

In 2 Corinthians 9:7, The Apostle Paul writes, *"Each of you should give what you have decided in your heart to give, not reluctantly or under compulsion, for God loves a cheerful giver."* God never forces a person to tithe, nor should anyone else. God gave men a free will, so they would be able to love and obey Him freely. Therefore, He will never force a person to give, love, pray, or anything else for that matter. God's Word gives men wisdom and instructions about how to best live their lives, but the choice to discover the truth of God's Word is in our control. Today, we are to give God our tithe in the same way that Abraham cheerfully tithed to God. We are to give from a heart of faith and gratefulness.

Next, I want to be honest with you. When I first decided

to tithe, I never had enough money left over to do it comfortably and most likely neither will you. That is because we Americans spend everything we make. When our income goes up, so do our bills, so it's always going to take faith and self-discipline to tithe. I said self-discipline because you might have to choose to pay your tithe over going out to eat or buying yourself a treat. Therefore, for most people (including myself), learning how to tithe will be a process. Start where you are, and I know the Holy Spirit will encourage you to grow in your faith to give Him the whole tithe. Now let me teach the truth of God's Word.

The Tithe

Deuteronomy 14:12 says, *"Be sure to set aside a tenth of all that your fields produce each year."* The Israelites, being farmers, were to give God a tenth of *all* that their farms produced each year. In other words, when there was an increase. Today, we tithe on our increase as well, which can be a paycheck, an inheritance, or profits from a business venture.

People often ask if they should tithe on their income before or after deductions (taxes, retirement fund contributions, and health insurance). I did both at different points in my walk with the Lord. Paying your tithe should be about what you truly believe the Word of God teaches or what you believe the Holy Spirit is prompting you to do.

Robbing God

Malachi 3:8 says, "Will a mere mortal rob God? Yet you rob me. But you ask, 'How are we robbing you?' In tithes and offerings." If I were going to rob you of something, it would mean that it was yours to begin with. God is saying in this Scripture that the tithe is His. If you are a child of God, the first 10 percent of your income belongs to God.

Next, it tells you where your tithe should go: *"Bring the whole tithe into the [local] storehouse, that there may be food in my house."* Your tithe should go to where you are being fed the Word of God. If you are attending a church, your tithe needs to go there. God has decided that pastors and other full-time church workers should receive their living from the people who are under their care. I realize that there may be people who are unable to go to church because of medical reasons, and they are fed spiritually by watching TV preachers. This would be a reason to send your tithe away from your local church unless your local pastor visits your home to minister to you.

Promise of Protection

God promises that if you pay your tithes, He will *"prevent pests from devouring your crops."* Sickness, lost money, lost work – all of these are pests that can "devour" your income. If you are tithing, you have a right to this promise, and you need to claim it. Whenever my finances are taken from me through one of these pests, I ask God to restore my finances, and He does every time. There are many ways that God has restored my finances, such as someone giving me something for free or by not having to pay full price for an item.

Restored Money

In May, I bought an older car that had air- conditioning, but when I tried to use it in July, I discovered it wasn't working. So, I took the car to a repair shop and spent $200 to have it recharged. The air-conditioner worked for a week, but then it stopped producing cold air. As far as I was concerned, $200 had just gone up into the air, and I was not happy about it, even though I knew this could happen, because I had purchased an older car. As I prayed about it, I mentioned to God that due to the promise of the tithe, He had promised to protect my finances. Well, here is what happened next...

I was a wedding photographer at that time, and I had placed an order for an album that was at least a month overdue. I had already made one phone call to the company and weeks later had to make a second call. When I called the second time, the woman on the other end was extremely apologetic. I told her it was no problem, but she said, "No, you shouldn't have had to wait this long, and we are going to give this album to you for free." I replied that it wasn't necessary, but she insisted. After the phone call ended, it came to my mind that the cost of the album was exactly $200. God had restored my money, and my faith to tithe was strengthened.

Now here is part two of this story. My son, Stuart, had gone to a Bible college that was 700 miles away, and finances were going to be difficult to keep him there. In other words, this was going to be a faith venture. The first week he was there, he called home to tell me that his car had just been broken into and they had stolen his CD player, CDs, and brand-new camera. His broken window

151

and stolen goods added up to about $750.

When he told me this, I could hear the discouragement in his voice, and it discouraged me as well. Then I remembered the promise of the tithe, and after I shared my story of how the Lord had restored my lost goods, I said to him, "Stuart, you are a tither, and you need to ask God to restore the money you lost according to His promise." We prayed together, and I encouraged him to believe that God would restore his lost money.

After our phone call, Stuart created a log of all that was stolen, expecting God to restore it all. About four days later, he called to tell us that a fellow student, whom he had never met before, came up to him at school and said that he and his wife had noticed him the other day and felt led to give him something. Then, the student handed him an envelope and walked away. The envelope contained $300. Stuart couldn't contain his excitement. He continued to watch for how the Lord would restore the balance and shared that all had been restored within two weeks of his prayer. This experience convinced Stuart that this was just the beginning of the miraculous provision he would need to keep him in that school, which it was.

Offerings

Your offerings may go where you feel the Holy Spirit is leading you to give. Many ministries are doing good works for God, and they need our support. Give to them without fear of going without. I have never been able to out-give God. In Luke 6:38, Jesus said, *"Give, and it will be given to you. A good measure, pressed down, shaken together and running over, will be poured into your lap. For with the measure you use, it will be measured to you."*

We *pay* our tithes, but we *give* our offerings. Our tithe is 10%, which has already been measured. The offerings we give are yet to be measured, and I believe it's the measure of our offerings that God uses to determine our increase.

Responsibility of a Married Spouse to Tithe

Many times, a married Christian wants to tithe, but their spouse isn't in agreement. They should tithe on what God has given them. What has God put into your hands? A paycheck? An allowance? You are only asked to tithe on what is yours.

Testing God's Word

Finally, God tells His people to *"test Him in this."* God's Word, when tested, will always prove itself to be true. Paying your tithe is not putting God to a foolish test. Not paying your tithe is foolish. I would rather have 90 percent of my income blessed than have 100 percent not protected by God's promise to prevent the *pests* from devouring my crops. Proverbs 3:9-10 says, *"Honor the Lord with your wealth, with the **first fruits** of all your crops; **then** your barns will be filled to overflowing, and your vats will brim over with new wine."* (emphasis added) God wants the first fruits, not your leftovers.

Paying my tithe demonstrates my faith in God's Word. It also humbly acknowledges my dependence upon Him to care for me. *"Give us today our daily bread."*

Risk Taking

When you first decide to start living life God's way, you may experience some amount of fear, depending on what you are trusting God to do for you. If that is so, your decision to act on God's Word will require some amount of risk taking. But your fear will lessen with each successful experience you have in discovering that God can be trusted to do what He said He would do.

I can assure you that God's future for you will be more exciting than you can imagine as you commit to following Him in obedience. I have discovered God's Holy Spirit to be patient, gentle, and an excellent teacher. So, enjoy this journey, you are on to discover God's abundant ways.

God's Spiritual Law of Increase

Proverbs 11:24-25, says, *"One person gives freely, yet gains even more; another withholds unduly, but comes to poverty. A generous person will prosper; whoever refreshes others will be refreshed."*

It goes against human logic to believe that when you give freely, you will gain even more. However, the way God accomplishes things in His kingdom is not like our ways or the ways of this world. Among church members, there's an old saying that goes, "you cannot out-give God." In other words, no matter how much you give to God, He will give you back even more. I have repeated this saying to myself every time my giving goes against my logic, to convince myself that I will not be hurt by giving away my goods. Goods I think I need. Afterward, when I could see that I had not been hurt in any way through my giving, it frees me to give the next time

154

without fearing lack.

Starting a Business

2 Corinthians 9:6, says, *"Remember this: Whoever sows sparingly will also reap sparingly, and whoever sows generously will also reap generously."*

I went to work for a short time while my children were still young. Erwin, an older gentleman from our church, offered to watch my children for me under one condition. He asked that all the money due him would go to Christian charities of his choice. I agreed and was blessed by his giving attitude.

Years later, I was once again a stay-at-home mom, cash-strapped because of my choice not to work outside of my home. I was 38-years old and tired of going without, so I took on an after-school childcare job. I was paid a small amount weekly, and I spent it on whatever I wanted to.

I enjoyed it for about six months when a missionary from Mexico City came to speak at our church. He ran a Sunday school program that also fed about 50,000 children each week. My heart was grieved as I heard him say that some of these children had to find their food in the garbage dump, called Garbage City, where they lived. After he finished speaking, the church took an offering to go towards feeding the children. I was so moved over his work that I decided to do as my friend Erwin had done, and I committed to God 100% of my childcare money to support this and the work of other missionaries. Afterward, I asked God if He would graciously increase my new photography business so I could still enjoy some

155

extra spending money.

Soon after I had decided to give God all of my childcare earnings, I decided to take another part-time job so I could afford to advertise my new photography business. The day I received my first paycheck, I was watching a Christian TV program. The TV preacher looked at the television audience and said, "There's someone out there who is going to start a business, and you are going to try to do it the world's way. Don't do it. Do it according to God's principles and only according to His principles." I knew God was speaking to me. He was telling me to take the money I had planned to spend on advertising and give it to Him instead. I did as He told me and increased my giving as I could.

Five years later, the Holy Spirit spoke to my heart. He asked me to get out my tax records for the last five years, so He could show me what He had done. Immediately, I noticed that the second year's financial bottom line was double what the first year's bottom line was. I kept looking and realized that God had doubled my income each year for the past five years. Even though I knew my business had been blessed, I was shocked to see how much my income had increased in such a short period of time. This outcome caused me to become even more convinced in my belief that we can't out-give God. He always gives us more to enable us to give again. *"You will be enriched in every way so that you can be generous on every occasion."* (2 Corinthians 9:11)

Seed Planting

Galatians 6:7 says, *"Do not be deceived: God cannot be mocked.*

A man reaps what he sows." The principle of sowing and reaping is as unchangeable as the law of gravity. It's also as sure as the law of gravity. What goes up must come down, and what a man sows is also what he shall reap. This is good news if you have been sowing good seeds. It's not such good news if you have been sowing bad seeds.

Let's look at seed planting or farming for a moment. The first time I heard this teaching was from Oral Roberts. It was the best teaching I had ever heard, and I immediately put it into practice. According to the law of sowing and reaping, when a farmer plants a corn seed, he knows that at harvest time he will reap more corn. He will never reap carrots if he has planted corn. Do you need to be loved? Be loving. Do you need a friend? Be a friend. Are you hateful? Be ready to receive hate. It is the same with finances. Do you need money? Then you need to give money. Give and it shall be given unto you. What shall be given to you? The "it" is what you gave. What you gave is also what shall be given to you.

Next, the amount of corn a farmer reaps depends upon how much seed he had planted. 2 Corinthians 9 says that if a man sows generously, he will also reap generously. Paul was talking about money here. This Scripture was given to the Corinthian people to encourage them to give financially to God's work. So, if you need to reap a large financial harvest, then you need to plant enough seeds to get a large harvest. Keep in mind that the measure you use to give is determined by what you currently possess and not by what someone else possesses. Jesus said that the widow who gave her two coins gave more (in measurement) than all the rich men had (Mark 12:42).

Additionally, as any farmer knows, you need to plant your seed in good soil. In Matthew, chapter 13, Jesus told the story of seeds falling onto four different kinds of ground. It was the seed that fell on good soil that was multiplied thirty, sixty, or a hundredfold. You must carefully choose the ministry that will receive your seed offering, as that's the ground you are planting your seed into. A ministry with good soil teaches good doctrine. It will also exalt God and not a man. Pray and ask the Holy Spirit to reveal to you where your offerings should go.

After the seed is planted, it must go through a death process. John 12:24 says, *"...Unless a kernel of wheat falls to the ground and dies, it remains only a single seed. But if it dies, it produces many seeds."* When you give, you must take your hands off the gift, because it's no longer yours. You cannot control the gift after you have given it. You also must not receive any direct benefit from your gift. It must be dead to you. Only then will God cause it to multiply.

After the farmer has planted his seed in good soil, he must then wait for it to grow. Ecclesiastes 11:1 tells us to, *"Cast your bread on the surface of the waters, for you will find it after many days."* (NASB) There is a growing season that must take place. Don't get impatient and quit on your harvest. Trust God to make it grow. Galatians 6:9 says, *"Let us not lose heart in doing good, for in due time we will reap if we do not grow weary."* (NASB) There's a due season, and we must wait for it.

When the harvest comes in, a farmer reserves seeds from that harvest, so he can plant next year's crop. DO NOT EAT ALL YOUR HARVEST. You need to enjoy the fruit of your labor to encourage you to work again, but you also need to reserve a portion to replant and start the process all over again. 2 Corinthians 9:10-11 says God, *"...Who supplies seed to the sower and bread for food will also supply and increase your store of seed and will enlarge the harvest of your righteousness. You will be enriched in every way so that you can be generous on every occasion."* This Scripture explains how it's God who gives you more seed to plant and causes them to grow, to enable you to be *generous on every occasion*. When you genuinely believe this, it will free you to be generous on every occasion without fearing lack.

For more information on Barbara's fashions, books, or speaking engagements, go to
www.daretodreamoncemore.com
Or: www.barbarakeisman.com

Made in the USA
Monee, IL
14 August 2021